SECOND EDITION

TEXT COMPLEXITY

SECOND EDITION

TEXT COMPLEXITY

STRETCHING READERS WITH TEXTS AND TASKS

DOUGLAS **FISHER**

NANCY **FREY**

DIANE **LAPP**

A JOINT PUBLICATION

CORWIN LITERACY

INTERNATIONAL LITERACY ASSOCIATION

FOR INFORMATION:

Corwin

A SAGE Company

2455 Teller Road

Thousand Oaks, California 91320

(800) 233-9936

www.corwin.com

SAGE Publications Ltd.

1 Oliver's Yard

55 City Road

London EC1Y 1SP

United Kingdom

SAGE Publications India Pvt. Ltd.

B 1/I 1 Mohan Cooperative Industrial Area

Mathura Road, New Delhi 110 044

India

SAGE Publications Asia-Pacific Pte. Ltd.

3 Church Street

#10-04 Samsung Hub

Singapore 049483

Publisher: Lisa Luedeke

Editorial Development Manager: Julie Nemer

Editorial Assistant: Nicole Shade

Production Editor: Melanie Birdsall

Copy Editor: Melinda Masson

Typesetter: C&M Digitals (P) Ltd.

Proofreader: Caryne Brown

Indexer: Jeanne R. Busemeyer

Cover Designer: Janet Kiesel

Marketing Manager: Rebecca Eaton

Printed in the United States of America

Library of Congress Cataloging-in-Publication Data

Names: Fisher, Douglas, author. | Frey, Nancy, author. | Lapp, Diane, author.

Title: Text complexity : stretching readers with texts and tasks / Douglas Fisher, Nancy Frey, Diane Lapp.

Description: Second edition. | Thousand Oaks, California : Corwin, 2016. | Includes bibliographical references and index.

Identifiers: LCCN 2015041812 | ISBN 978-1-5063-3944-3 (pbk. : alk. paper)

Subjects: LCSH: Reading comprehension.

Classification: LCC LB1573.7 .F56 2016 | DDC 372.47—dc23 LC record available at http://lccn.loc.gov/2015041812

This book is printed on acid-free paper.

SUSTAINABLE FORESTRY INITIATIVE

Certified Chain of Custody
Promoting Sustainable Forestry
www.sfiprogram.org
SFI-01268

SFI label applies to text stock

16 17 18 19 20 10 9 8 7 6 5 4 3 2 1

Contents

Preface

If you're previewing this preface with the question of what has changed since we published the first edition of *Text Complexity*, the answer is quite simple: our response to the empowered voices of educators who are asking more detailed questions about their roles in preparing students to read complex texts across the disciplines. With a renewed belief that students who are prepared to succeed must be able to read well and extensively, write from a base of information, and speak clearly in ways that hold the attention of listeners, teachers are intent on crafting purposeful instruction that results in all students becoming literate across the grades and subjects.

State and national calls for students to learn how to deeply comprehend and evaluate informational and literary texts—and also how to craft multiple text types that are needed for career and social success—have been sounded, and as a result, everyone is looking to the teacher as never before to ensure that all students leave school with college- and workplace-ready skills. A widening awareness that literacy is the linchpin for success in school and the future workplace has grasped the attention of teachers across grade levels and disciplines who are attempting to ensure literacy learning without losing the veracity of their disciplines.

We work with hundreds of educators across the country and are privy to their questions:

- What features of a text constitute complexity?
- How do these features differ across the grades and disciplines?
- How can we support all students in mastering the literacy skills needed to read increasingly complex texts?

Focusing on teachers' concerns, we updated and recast this second edition with information and examples designed to provide instruction that supports making written text accessible to all. We have expanded this edition from five to nine chapters that retain an easy-to-read tone, a clear structure, and lots of classroom scenarios. The focus remains on text complexity across a number of dimensions, including quantitative factors and qualitative text features, but we have expanded our emphasis on reader and task considerations.

In **Chapter 1**, we discuss text complexity. We also discuss the struggles readers face uncovering the deepest meaning of a text and the power of these struggles. We explore the role teachers play in planning and assessing instruction that involves students in tasks requiring analysis of a wide array of textual information.

Chapter 2 focuses on identifying the quantifiable or countable features of a text such as word length, number of appearances, and sentence length. For decades, these were the sole features used to determine a text's readability level. Continued study of challenging texts has made obvious that features that can be quantified represent only *one* dimension of a text's complexity and that its qualitative features must also be considered.

Consideration of the qualitative features of a text, the ones that invite an analysis of meaning, language, structure, and author intent, must also be weighted heavily in determining text complexity. But this cannot occur in isolation either. The readers who will be reading the text and the tasks they will be asked to perform must be considered, too. In the first edition of this text, only one chapter addressed issues related to qualitative features; however, we believe it is essential to analyze informational and literary texts with greater precision. In fact, understanding how to assess the qualitative features in both informational and literary texts is so essential to making a match between readers and texts that we have devoted **Chapters 3** *and* **4** to this discussion in this new edition.

The complexities of literary texts having narrative plot-driven structures and those illustrating point of view and imagery are discussed in **Chapter 3**. A rubric is included to support analysis of levels of meaning and purpose, structure, language conventionality and clarity, and knowledge demands. The information that can be gleaned by assessing a text against criteria identified in the rubric can help you identify the reader–text relationship and where instruction should be focused.

In **Chapter 4**, characteristics of informational texts that describe, inform, and explain information are described. A second complexity scale for analysis of informational texts is new to this book. This scale was developed at the urging of teacher-colleagues who found the qualitative scale shared in Chapter 3 in the first edition to be useful for analyzing literary texts but struggled with using it with informational texts. The scale shared in Chapter 4 encourages complexity analysis through the lens of field, tenor, and mode and is the result of our teacher-colleagues' insights. Discussion and examples are included that illustrate how to use this scale to analyze an informational text. Again, this analysis should always occur with the readers for whom the text is being selected and the tasks they will be asked to perform in mind.

Chapters 5 through 9 focus on teaching complex texts and guiding students' learning from those texts. We have expanded this section from two to five chapters in this edition, with new chapters focusing on teacher modeling, close reading, scaffolded reading, collaborative learning, and independent reading. While some of these topics were introduced in the first edition, the emphasis in this new edition is on the interactive role played by teachers and students in learning to read complex texts. Teachers make text selections for the instructional purposes they have identified, assess the areas that will be complex for their students, teach students how to notice what is confusing for them, and then provide instruction that eliminates these areas of confusion. In the process, students learn how to empower themselves as independent readers. Chapters 5 through 9 introduce instruction ensuring that students develop competence and confidence as readers.

Chapter 5 describes the power and practice of teacher modeling as an effective tool for building students' reading proficiency and skill. Examples illustrate how a proficient reader employs a cognitive strategy such as visualizing, inferring, summarizing, predicting, questioning, or monitoring to make sense of a text, and how a proficient reader grapples with an unknown word or phrase. These examples across the disciplines illustrate disciplinary experts employing the habits of a reader in a specific discipline.

Since publication of the first edition of this text, much attention has been focused on the close reading approach. In **Chapter 6**, we discuss the features of a close reading lesson and provide scenarios of teachers engaging students in close reading experiences. Text-dependent questions play a powerful role during a close reading. Questions that move readers to consider what the text says, its structure, and the author's intentions are shared through discussion and example. The power and necessity of collaboration as a dimension of close reading are also illustrated in this chapter and addressed in much greater detail in Chapter 8.

In **Chapter 7**, we discuss the importance of scaffolded reading for building the capacity of readers to engage with increasingly complex texts.

Here, we emphasize the texts selected and the instructional intentions of the teacher regarding scaffolds, which are essential to enabling students to stretch and grapple with texts that are more difficult than ones that they can access independently. We also describe and discuss scaffolded small-group reading instruction as an extension of close reading.

As mentioned earlier, in **Chapter 8** we focus on the power of collaborating with peers while reading challenging texts. But we must put into place supports that ensure students become successful collaborators. We realize that peer talk is a suggestion often met with trepidation because we all have fears of talk getting off task and volume increasing to an off-task level. Conditions that support peer-led collaboration include providing tasks and procedures for teaching students to collaborate. We share many examples in Chapter 8 of teachers implementing routines and practices that support inviting students to communicate about the complex texts they are reading. We believe engaging students in purposeful talk about a text is an essential component of understanding the text.

Teaching students to read well should not be the final goal of a teacher. Rather, a teacher's final goal should be to instill in students a desire to read independently across subjects. In **Chapter 9**, we share ideas for building a reader's strength, stamina, and desire. Like you, we believe that being a strong and avid reader in and out of school is a significant factor in having a successful life. We wish this for every student, and we hope that the ideas we have shared in this second edition help you to support every student in becoming more skilled at reading complex texts.

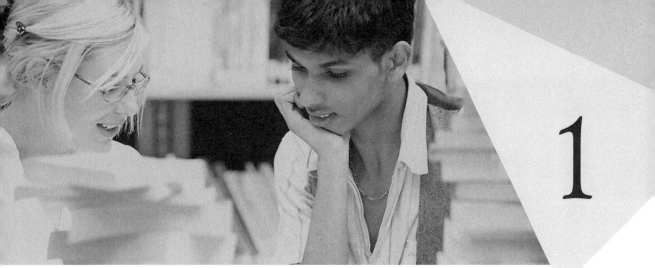

Text Complexity in a New Light

Who would have expected *Charlotte's Web*, the beloved children's classic by E. B. White, first published in 1952, to become so controversial? This book seems to have become the so-called line in the sand, pitting elementary educators against one another. Should its home continue to reside in fourth grade, where it has been traditionally used? Is it better used as a third-grade book, given its 680 Lexile score? Or maybe it should be in second grade, where it could serve as a way to stretch the comprehension of younger students. Or is it best used with first graders as a read-aloud and discussion text? We've variously encountered fourth-grade teachers in tears because they've been told they can't order copies, second-grade teachers who view it apprehensively because it exceeds the reading level of many children that age, first-grade teachers trying to plan lessons on listening comprehension, and third-grade teachers trying to figure out what time of year they should introduce it. So which is it—is *Charlotte's Web* a first-, second-, third-, or fourth-grade book? Our answer is that the book belongs in all of these grades, depending on what you want to do with it.

Admittedly, that answer is sometimes met with frustration, but it shines a spotlight on how the topic of text complexity is being shaped in the years since new standards were first introduced. Regardless of the state, territory, or country where you teach, expectations about the reading levels of students are a topic of continuing concern. Definitions of text complexity, and the implications they hold for instruction, have permeated discussions about reading development. What was once the concern of a subset of researchers and specialists is now the topic of grade-level meetings and professional development workshops for practitioners.

However, with renewed attention on text complexity has come a shift in what should be considered when determining the suitability of texts for different students and different tasks. The attention given to quantitative measures in particular has resulted in less attention on other factors, specifically the interaction between the reader and the task, with the text characteristics serving as an intermediary between the two (Valencia, Wixson, & Pearson, 2014). The purpose of this book is to expand on text complexity and how it impacts the instructional and assessment decisions educators make for students. In doing so, we allot more literary real estate (and thus attention) to considerations about the reader and the task. In subsequent chapters, we discuss quantitative measures, then turn our attention to qualitative values. We believe that the teacher's understanding of the qualitative values in particular is essential to designing meaningful tasks. The second half of the book, new to this edition, comprises five chapters devoted to the tasks we design for our students to enable their understanding of a range of texts.

In this chapter, we provide an overview of text complexity before turning our attention to the central factor when considering text complexity: the reader. This is where all of us begin and end every teaching decision we make. Therefore, this first chapter of a book about text complexity contains extensive information about the reader and the task demand. We then introduce pathways for selecting texts that vary based on your point of entry, and unpack the technical aspects of analyzing texts quantitatively and qualitatively such that it yields practical and actionable results.

▶ Untangling Terminology

While participating in, and listening to, the discussions about texts and students, we often hear three terms being used interchangeably: *text complexity*, *readability*, and *difficulty*. These three concepts are closely related, but are not quite synonymous, which in turn leads to misinterpretations. *Text complexity*, the subject of this book, is multidimensional and challenges us to consider four facets:

- The quantitative and qualitative features of the text itself
- The characteristics of the reader utilizing the text
- What the reader is tasked with doing with the text
- The *readability* of the text. This is a subset of text complexity, and concerns itself primarily with the *quantitative* measures of the text, such as
  - Sentence length
  - Syntax
  - Vocabulary
  - Number of rare words

Readability is calculated using a formula, and primarily analyzes the surface levels of the text. We expand on readability formulas and other quantitative measures in the next chapter.

Difficulty is another subset of text complexity and describes the interaction between the reader and the text. It is how manageable the text is going to be for an individual reader. Text difficulty is affected by a number of factors, including interest, motivation, and the relative fit between the reader's knowledge base and the amount needed to comprehend the text. These factors overlap somewhat with other elements of text complexity and include the amount of effort a reader must expend to achieve an acceptable level of accuracy, fluency, and comprehension of the text. For example, a graduate-level physics textbook would pose a higher-than-acceptable level of text difficulty for the three of us, when compared to a student enrolled in the course.

▶ Text Complexity Expanded

In order to drill down a bit further into the concept of text complexity, we have to discuss the intersection between reading comprehension and text. In 2002, the RAND Reading Study Group released an influential report advising researchers on future directions in literacy research. As part of that report, they developed a heuristic for thinking about the factors that affect reading comprehension and the various ways they intersect with one another. They defined reading comprehension as the "process of simultaneously extracting and constructing meaning through interaction and involvement with written language" (p. xiii) and identified three elements—reader, activity, and text—that are embedded within sociocultural contexts. These sociocultural contexts represent the reader's lived experiences both in and out of school that influence how texts and ideas are understood (see Figure 1.1).

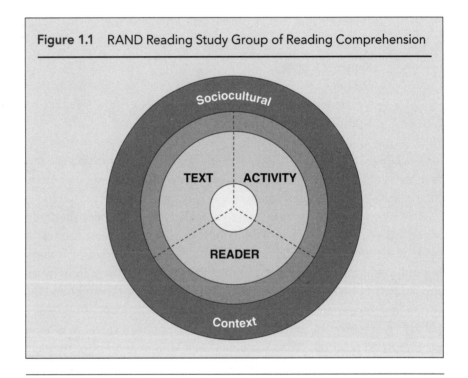

Figure 1.1   RAND Reading Study Group of Reading Comprehension

Source: RAND Reading Study Group (2002).

The work of the RAND Reading Study Group in turn influenced the architects of the Common Core State Standards (CCSS) in defining text complexity through a three-part model:

1. The qualitative dimensions of text complexity such as purpose and meaning that are identified by a human reader

2. The quantitative dimensions of text complexity such as sentence length and text cohesion that are measured by a computer

3. Reader and task considerations, which are best known to the teacher (National Governors Association Center for Best Practices & Council of Chief State School Officers, 2010b; see Figure 1.2)

Figure 1.2   CCSS Text Complexity

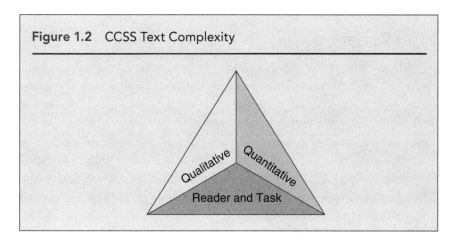

Source: National Governors Association Center for Best Practices & Council of Chief State School Officers (2010b).

We offer Figures 1.1 and 1.2 for comparison purposes, and to restate a fact that is easily missed when the details are overlooked in favor of an overall impression: the importance of the reader and the task should not take a backseat to the text. That is to say not that understanding the text is insignificant, but rather that the relationship between reader and task is critical (Valencia et al., 2014).

Quantitative measures, including readability formulas, calculate the surface features of a text, such as sentence length, syntax, and types of words used to yield a numeral value. Some quantitative measures are scaled such that a reader's skill level is correlated to a particular quantitative value, as with Lexile measures (Smith, Stenner, Horabin, & Smith, 1989). We examine these in more depth in Chapter 2. Qualitative values, on the other hand, are used to describe elements that are less easily scored through a counting function, especially in examining levels of meaning and purposes, the use or absence of language conventions, the overall knowledge demand of the piece, and the structures used.

There is some overlap in what each measure reports. To varying degrees, each identifies the characteristics of a text that can pose a challenge to a reader: the semantic and syntactic structures, vocabulary load, organization, and linguistic features such as parts of speech and cohesion among sentences. The primary variable is not what is analyzed but rather how it is analyzed. Each methodology measures some things exceedingly well, and yet each is inadequate on its own for measuring other aspects of text complexity.

▶ The Reader

Ultimately, it is the reader who is the arbiter of a text, who in turn is shaped by the tasks that accompany the text. To overlook the transaction that occurs between the reader and the task as it relates to the text would allow for a serious miscalculation. It is analogous to looking at the Grand Canyon from only one viewpoint. You can see a slice, maybe even a meaningful portion, but you can't truly appreciate its dimensions until you have seen it from above, from below, and at various points in between. Knowledge of the reader requires understanding his or her

Ultimately, it is the reader who is the arbiter of a text. To overlook the transaction that occurs between the reader and the task as it relates to the text would allow for a serious miscalculation.

1. Cognitive capabilities
2. Motivation
3. Background knowledge
4. Experiences

We describe each of these considerations further, as follows.

Cognitive Capabilities

Whereas the passage from the RAND report locates cognitive capabilities within the reader, we take a broader view of this concept to include our own capacity as teachers to utilize and extend these factors. Understanding who the reader is makes us capable of choosing the right text for the right student and pair it with the right instructional task.

Attention and memory are key cognitive variables in reading. Visual attention to print is essential in the development of reading but not a given among emergent readers. Studies of young children engaged in storybook reading have found that they attend to print 3–7 percent of the time, spending most of it looking at the pictures. However, when an adult prompted the children's attention through verbal inquiries and gestures, the time the children spent attending to the print increased significantly (Justice, Pullen, & Pence, 2008). Asking them "Can you show me the letter *b* in this word?" while pointing to the speech bubble on a page with dialogue or tracking the print with a finger while reading nearly doubled the amount of time these young children spent attending to print.

Interestingly, the researchers found that the nonverbal interactions resulted in more fixations on print than the verbal ones did. The authors further projected that for a child who is read to for ten minutes a day, this would result in eighteen thousand more fixations on print in the course of one year. The growing ability of a reader to attend to text is directly related to one's working memory capacity (sometimes incorrectly called short-term memory). All readers temporarily store letters and words to manipulate them so they can be decoded and assigned meaning (Kintsch & Van Dijk, 1978). Attention and working memory are executive functions, meaning that the reader is able to influence them to some degree. However, background knowledge, prior experiences, and vocabulary knowledge are also factors, perhaps explaining up to 66 percent of the variance between readers with strong comprehension skills and those who struggle to understand (Cromley & Azevedo, 2007). Working memory for reading comprehension is further strengthened by the conscious choice to limit intrusive thoughts (i.e., mind wandering) so the reader can maintain focus on the passage (McVay & Kane, 2011). In the same way that our instructional practices can positively influence young students' attention to print, we can direct the attention of older readers by clearly establishing purpose for them before they read (Fisher & Frey, 2011). There are, of course, variations among children. Students who are learning English must divide their attention and working memory to make meaning (Thomas, Healy, & Greenberg, 2007).

Some readers have identified language or learning differences that require us to provide more specialized supports. Others have fewer formal language experiences than their classmates. However, variances among the students in our classrooms cannot result in lowered expectations for their learning, especially by systematically denying them access to the kinds of rich text experiences of others (e.g., Elliott, 2015). Instead, we must find ways to scaffold their reading experiences by differentiating instruction and providing accommodations and modifications as warranted. These are teaching concepts that we have known for decades, and increased expectations for reading should not be seen as a retreat from these practices.

Motivation

A student who is motivated to read something can far exceed our expectations of what he or she should be capable of reading. We have witnessed adolescents labeled as struggling readers who pore over technical manuals and blogs discussing the subject they're interested in reading about. Many of us have known a younger child who can seemingly digest an informational book about a topic of acute interest to him or her—poisonous spiders, horses, or space exploration—and discuss this in detail with others. A motivated reader is one who engages in significantly more reading than one who is not motivated to do so. Wigfield and Guthrie (1997) have identified a 300 percent difference in time spent reading between intrinsically motivated and unmotivated fourth- and fifth-grade readers. Although we don't expect young students to identify their college and career plans, we notice these sparks of interest among our students and place interesting (and, yes, complex) texts in their paths. When we do so, students engage with texts for hours.

However, our concern is that the concept of intrinsic motivation gets confounded with the character traits of the actual reader. We assert that intrinsic motivation in students is largely influenced by situational conditions and that even highly motivated readers can find their enthusiasm dampened because of circumstances. Nancy recalls a time when she briefly joined an adult book club (something she was highly motivated to do) only to quickly discover that one person in the group controlled all the conversations, interrupted others, and cut people off when they disagreed with her. In short order, Nancy became a book club dropout, even though her interest in the book itself remained high.

In large part, instructional practices can contribute to, or detract from, a student's motivation to read. In their review of the role of motivation in reading, McRae and Guthrie (2009) have identified five teaching practices that foster motivation, and five that destroy it. The following instructional practices impact motivation positively:

1. Relevance
2. Choice
3. Success
4. Collaboration
5. Thematic units

Avoid these five practices because they have a negative effect:

1. Nonrelevance
2. Excessive control

3. Difficult lessons
4. Frequent individual work
5. Disconnected units

Teachers strongly influence these elements of curricular organization and social interactions. Organization of the curriculum is largely responsible for the degree to which we can ground relevance by establishing purpose in lessons, in the ways we design units to promote further investigation of a topic, and in how we foster choice within those investigations (Fisher & Frey, 2011). In addition, instruction should be aligned with the principles of social interaction as a necessary condition of learning. To propel learning forward, we need students to engage in incrementally more demanding (but not impossible) tasks—in the company of others who are learning and with expert guidance close at hand when the group gets stuck.

We add one more dimension to this list: goal setting. It is important to note that motivation is not limited to interest or enjoyment of the task itself. We think of the athlete who spends many hours in isolation, hitting baseballs or shooting free throws. The motivation in these cases is not that the task is so enjoyable but rather that the athlete recognizes that putting in the hours of practice will result in improved performance. Ericsson, Krampe, and Tesch-Römer (1993) call this deliberate practice the "repeated experiences in which the individual can attend to the critical aspects of the situation and incrementally improve her or his performance in response to knowledge of results, feedback, or both from a teacher" (p. 368). Teachers can promote deliberate practice through goal setting with students when they link goal-setting activities back to the established purposes. In other words, goal setting should be a regular part of the instructional design process.

> We need students to engage in demanding (but not impossible) tasks—in the company of others who are learning and with expert guidance close at hand.

Background Knowledge

All texts place a certain amount of knowledge demand on a reader, if for no other reason than that even the simplest text can't fully explain every detail. ("Old MacDonald had a farm. Old MacDonald is the name of the farmer. A farmer raises animals and crops. Crops are edible plants grown on large plots of land. . . ." You get the idea.) Yet possession of requisite knowledge is insufficient. Learners must also be practiced at accessing that information. This is where novices falter—they are not especially good at using needed information to understand newer knowledge. The competition for attention is just too great. In an effort to attend to new information, they temporarily forget about other cognitive resources that they otherwise know. In other words, it's a question not so much of whether they possess the necessary prior knowledge and background experiences but of whether they are able to marshal these resources when needed.

Accessing known knowledge requires the reader to be able to engage in metacognitive thinking. Thinking about one's thinking is essential for pairing the known with the unknown (Donovan & Bransford, 2005) and is a critical factor in distinguishing a novice from an expert (Ericsson & Charness, 1994). A dimension of metacognition is self-management, explained by Cross and Paris (1988) as consisting of the following three categories: evaluation, planning, and regulation. In the context of reading, evaluation refers to analyses of task characteristics and personal abilities that affect comprehension. Planning involves the selection of particular strategies for reaching the goals that have been set or chosen. Regulation is the monitoring and redirection of one's activities during the course of reading to reach the desired goals.

Further, their work with third- and fifth-grade readers found that instruction about metacognitive thinking led to increased comprehension and performance, most notably among students who were identified as reading below grade level. As with other factors about the reader, metacognitive knowledge is not innate and static, but can be directly influenced through purposeful instruction.

Experiences

Of all the factors we have discussed regarding the reader, his or her experiences may appear to be the most far removed from our influence. It is true that you cannot rewind the clock to make sure that students were exposed to rich interactive language when they were babies or that they were regularly read to as toddlers. However, we can capitalize on their current experiences, if we are intentional about it. In other words, it is not simply having the experience, but rather how that experience is leveraged to understand text. For example, field trips and other out-of-class excursions are a regular feature of school but are not always used as fruitfully as they could be in reading development. To do so, students should be reading related texts in advance of a field trip to build topical knowledge and also afterward to deepen and extend their understanding. In a personal communication with a colleague, an assistant superintendent who was struggling with her staff to make field trips more relevant, she said, "They don't need to see the ocean to learn how to read. But if they go to see the ocean, they need to read as much about it as possible before and after their experience."

A kindergarten trip to the local zoo might include shared readings of books like *'Twas the Day Before Zoo Day* by Catherine Ipcizade (2008) or *I Want to Be a Zookeeper* by Daniel Liebman (2003) before students travel there. After this experience, students are ready for more complex texts, such as *Zoo* by Gail Gibbons (1991) and Aliki's (1997) *My Visit to the Zoo*. In this way, both texts and experiences are coordinated to scaffold students' understanding of more complex texts.

The knowledge a reader has acquired is an amalgam of developmental growth, instruction, motivations, and experiences. A checklist for exploring these factors can be found in Figure 1.3. All are brought to bear to comprehend text. However, teachers design tasks to act as a catalyst to advance comprehension beyond what a child is able to do in the absence of any instruction. In other words, the level of complexity doesn't reside solely within the four corners of the page. The task, and the reader's capacity to take on the task, shapes text complexity.

Figure 1.3 Checklist for Considering Characteristics of Readers: Exploring the Reader

Cognitive Capabilities	Notes
Will this text maintain the student's attention?	
Will this text tax the reader's working memory?	
Will this text require specialized supports (e.g., language support, accommodations)?	
Does this text contain enough supports to move the reader forward in learning rather than cause frustration?	
Motivation	**Notes**
Does the topic or genre of the text interest the reader?	

(Continued)

Figure 1.3 (Continued)

Motivation (Continued)	Notes
Is the text relevant to the reader?	
Does the reader have an opportunity to exercise choice?	
Has the reader experienced success in the past with this topic or genre?	
Does the student have opportunities to collaborate with others before and after the reading?	
Is the text being used to connect to larger themes or concepts?	
Will this text allow the reader to meet a goal he or she has set?	
Knowledge	**Notes**
Does the reader possess specialized knowledge about the topic or genre?	
Does the reader possess the needed metacognitive skills to comprehend the text?	
Does the reader have sufficient background and/or prior knowledge to link to new information?	
Experiences	**Notes**
What direct experiences does the reader have that may make this text more accessible?	
Is this text more complex than previous ones, in order to build the reader's skills and knowledge?	

▶ The Reader Meets the Task

The writer of a text always presumes a reader's knowledge. A reference guide written for pharmacists, such as *Drug Interactions Analysis and Management 2014* by Philip Hansten and John Horn (2014), presumes a high degree of prior knowledge on the part of its reader. Conversely, *The Pill Book* by Harold Silverman (2012), with its photographs, extensive glossary, and subheadings (e.g., "Prescribed For," "Cautions and Warnings," "Possible Side Effects"), is specifically written for the layperson, one who does not possess advanced training in the subject. Judging by their longevity (the first is in its ninth edition, the second in its fifteenth), both do their jobs exceedingly well. Yet a pharmacist would be frustrated by the lack of technical information in *The Pill Book*, whereas the worried parent of a four-year-old breaking out in a strange rash after switching to a new cough syrup would be confused by the information in *Drug Interactions Analysis and Management 2014*. Neither book is better or worse than the other; they simply vary in the amount of knowledge required to understand them. For that reason, they are appropriate for different audiences.

Readers read for a variety of purposes, and all of us like to read texts that are comfortable for us, especially when we are looking for new information. In each case in the previous scenario, the purpose, and thus the task, differed. In this case, each reader needed to find the text that best met the task at hand. For example, when Doug was asked to develop a new online class and not simply use discussion boards and postings, he searched for some reading material that would help him with this task. *The Exceptional Presenter Goes Virtual* (Koegel, 2010) provided Doug with information that he could use and that he understood.

The overriding factor for designing the right task for the right reader is a social one: in whose company will the task be completed?

In terms of matching the reader and the task, Doug had the cognitive capability to read the selected text independently, he was motivated to learn more about the topic because of a task that he needed to complete, and his background knowledge included presenting, but not presenting in a virtual environment. In addition, because Doug was reading the book independently, the text needed to contain enough scaffolds for him to successfully work his way through the information without any other guidance. Had Doug been working in a group, the selected text could have been a more difficult one. Alternatively, Doug could have taken a class and worked with an experienced online teacher using a still more challenging text.

Understanding these factors requires an exploration of the task required of the reader. Many elements contribute to task design, such as whether the task draws on a student's declarative knowledge (what to use), procedural knowledge (how to use it), or conditional knowledge (when to use it). In addition, students engaged in a task must make decisions about how to plan for the task, monitor progress, and correct errors. In fact, the subject of task design is so important that we have dedicated several chapters to it. But the overriding factor for designing the right task for the right reader is a social one: in whose company will the task be completed? In other words, is the task sufficiently complex such that it will need to be led by the teacher? Or is the task best achieved in the company of peers? Perhaps the task is one that will be done independently. We have created a preliminary checklist (Figure 1.4) to support initial identification of various features of a text-based task that highlight the teacher's role, the collaborative and social features of the task, and its potential to motivate and challenge the student(s).

Figure 1.4   Exploring the Task

Teacher-Led Tasks	Notes
Does this text require modeling of cognitive comprehension strategies?	
Does this text require modeling of word-solving strategies?	
Does this text require modeling of text structures?	
Does this text require modeling of text features?	
Peer Tasks	**Notes**
Does the task match the readers' collaborative learning skills?	

Peer Tasks (Continued)	Notes
Does the task match the readers' social skills?	
Does the task require that students engage in accountable talk?	
Are suitable supports for accountable talk (e.g., language frames) furnished?	

Individual Tasks	Notes
Does the task provide sufficient challenge for the student, while avoiding protracted frustration?	
Are the text and the task sufficiently more complex than previous ones, so that they provide opportunities to build the reader's skills and knowledge?	

Concerns about the ability of a reader to handle a text-based task are constant in the life of a classroom teacher. We're continually looking for that sweet spot—not too easy, yet not too hard—that will challenge but not defeat a reader. However, this has resulted in an overcorrection in the field. In an attempt to reduce defeat, we have eliminated productive struggle. Without opportunities to cognitively stretch a bit, students spend far too much time with comfortable text, and far less time with texts and tasks that afford moderate challenges. We don't want children to put their heads on their desks and weep in frustration. There is nothing to be accomplished when the tasks and texts are far out of reach. But struggle can be productive, when dished out carefully and monitored closely.

▶ The Case for Struggle

Perhaps one of the mistakes in the past efforts to improve reading achievement has been the removal of struggle. As a profession, we might have made reading tasks too easy. We are suggesting not that we plan students' failure, but rather that they be provided with opportunities to struggle, and to learn about themselves as readers when they do struggle, persevere, and eventually succeed. After all, pride comes from effort and success, not just completing easy tasks.

This concept of supportive struggle is known as productive failure (Kapur, 2008). Productive failure provides students an opportunity to struggle with something and learn from the mistakes that are made along the way. Again, it's not planned failure, but rather an opportunity to wrestle with some text for a bit and learn along the way. Consider the worthy struggle for a group of students reading the following from *Faithful Elephants*, recounting the bombing of Tokyo in the final months of World War II:

> What would happen if bombs hit the zoo? If the cages were broken and dangerous animals escaped to run wild through the city, it would be terrible! Therefore, by command of the Army, all of the lions, tigers, leopards, bears, and big snakes were poisoned to death. (Tsuchiya, 1951, p. 9)

Again, the individual words are not that hard (seventh-grade level), but the ideas are complex and tragic. As students talked about what the author said, and considered the time at which this was written, they struggled to figure out why the animals were killed. They used evidence from the text to justify their responses, such as when Justin said, "This is a memory from the guy at the memorial. He's remembering this. I think so because of how sad he was at the end and how he was taking care of the marker at the beginning."

Marla responded, "I agree with you. The title says that it's true, and I think that this was a time when they were worried about war and tried to protect people." Their conversation continued, and they struggled to understand a text written at a different time for a different audience. And through that struggle, they came to an understanding.

As one of the members of the group said, "Sometimes wars are necessary, but there are always bystanders hurt along the way. I never thought about the animals, but I guess that they are bystanders of human wars, too."

The struggle that comes from using texts that stretch students' capacity just a bit provides them with opportunities to become more skilled readers, not just strategic ones. Consider this early passage from the novel *Extremely Loud and Incredibly Close* (Foer, 2005):

> Anyway, the fascinating thing was that I read in *National Geographic* that there are more people alive now than have died in all of human history. In other words, if everyone wanted to play Hamlet at once, they couldn't, because there aren't enough skulls! (p. 3)

The above passage is hard for a number of different reasons. From a quantitative perspective, the novel is a 940 Lexile, placing it in the middle school band. From a qualitative perspective, there are assumptions about background knowledge hidden in this text. The reference to *National Geographic* signals most readers that the information is verifiable. Additionally, understanding the reference to Hamlet and the prop used in the famous soliloquy is critical to making meaning of the second sentence. But a reader could skip that referent and still get the gist of the text. What really makes this text hard is the central idea in these sentences, as the deep meaning comes from understanding the implications of the statement. The words themselves are not that difficult, but the mathematical computation is mind-boggling and causes most readers to pause and consider what the character is saying. We ask ourselves, could that be true? Did I just read that correctly? Is it hyperbole or fact? In doing so, we slowed down, and our fluency rate decreased, but our comprehension soared.

Developing readers need regular exposure to more complex texts so that they can experience acceptable levels of struggle.

When reading gets hard, readers slow down and try to make sense of the text. That's what happened when we read the passage that included *National Geographic* and Hamlet. It's not that the reader slows down so much as that he gets lost, but slows down enough to become strategic. But being strategic is not the goal of reading. Reading requires automaticity—the systematic and automatic deployment of cognitive behaviors to make meaning of the text. As readers become increasingly adept at deploying cognitive strategies automatically, they become skilled readers. As Afflerbach, Pearson, and Paris (2008) point out, "reading skills operate without the reader's deliberate control or conscious awareness . . . [t]his has important, positive consequences for each reader's limited working memory" (p. 368). Strategies, on the other hand, are "effortful and deliberate" and occur during initial learning, when the text is more difficult for the reader to understand (p. 369). Strategies become skills with instruction and practice, and practice occurs when readers encounter authentic situations in which they need to use these tools. In other words, developing readers need regular exposure to more complex texts so that they can experience acceptable levels of struggle that require them to deploy strategies for regaining comprehension. In doing so, over time readers will generalize their skills and become proficient readers who can read widely. But they will not learn to do so if they are always restricted to text that is comfortable and less challenging. To become skilled requires that readers struggle a bit as they apply these strategies in new situations, in time becoming more fluent at doing so. Figure 1.5 contains a summary of the differences between skills and strategies.

Figure 1.5   Comparing Skills and Strategies

Skill	Strategy
An automatic procedure that readers use unconsciously.	A conscious plan under the control of the reader.
Does not require thought, interpretation, or choice.	Requires thought about which strategies to use and when to use them.
Observable behaviors such as are found on taxonomies, skills tests, or answers to questions.	Process-oriented, cognitive procedures the reader uses, generally unobservable in nature.
Instruction focuses on repeated use until it becomes habitual.	Instruction focuses on the reasoning process readers use as they interact with text.

Source: Frey, Fisher, & Berkin (2009). Fisher, Douglas; Frey, Nancy; Berkin, Adam, *Good Habits, Great Readers: Building the Literacy Community,* 1st Ed. © 2009. Reprinted by permission of Pearson Education, Inc., New York, New York.

▶ Pathways for Selecting Texts

Think about all of the times you select texts in a given week. Chances are very good that your starting point varies, depending on your purpose. By that, we mean that the decision is borne out of one of several needs:

1. You have a wonderful piece of text that your students simply must experience. But you need to decide what to do with it.

2. You have identified an area of instructional need for a group of students (e.g., tracking extended dialogue between two characters) and need to find a text that provides the opportunity for students to learn the skill.

3. You need to locate a reading whose content will contribute to building the knowledge of your students about the topic, but it needs to be aligned to the instructional arrangement you'll use (e.g., teacher-led, student-led, or independent).

However, you're not done just because you have a text in hand. You need to identify your learning intentions for your students. Your purpose is further influenced by the results of the gap analysis you perform in considering the reader and the text. You'll recall that these include the reader's cognitive capabilities, motivation, knowledge, and experiences (Figure 1.3). And you'll take the text's qualitative and quantitative characteristics into consideration. Based on your gap analysis, you identify the task level that seems to best address the gap. For example, if the gap is significant, you may determine that teacher modeling and thinking aloud is needed, and may include further guided instruction in the form of a close reading. On the other hand, the gap might be better suited to collaborative reading with peers who can scaffold each other's understanding through discussion and shared tasks. If the gap is small, then an independent reading task is probably in order. But perhaps the problem is the text itself, as it doesn't align with the possible instructional support you can provide for this text.

Selecting a text is more than simply choosing a title from a list or a bookshelf. We are always considering the reader and the task. However, as Valencia et al. (2014) note, the characteristics of the reader are variables that a teacher is comparatively less able to manipulate, while the text selection and the task that accompanies it are well within the teacher's scope of influence. In fact, it is the relationship between the text and the task, rather than the characteristics of the text alone, that informs text complexity (Valencia et al., 2014). As noted previously, tasks encompass both what a student does cognitively and metacognitively and within what instructional arrangement he or she will learn this knowledge. For now, we will confine our decision-making paths to the instructional arrangement, and explore the cognitive and metacognitive tasks later in the book. These decision-making paths, which we reference through this text, can be found in Figure 1.6.

▶ Conclusion

Text complexity is an important consideration in literacy instruction. Students are expected to learn to read, and understand, increasingly complex texts as they get older. Texts can be analyzed both quantitatively and qualitatively, and teachers have to know their readers and the type of instruction that is likely to result in better reading. Deep knowledge of text complexity and instructional support, combined with a willingness to allow students to grapple with concepts, words, and ideas, puts teachers and students on the path to success. Failure to understand text complexity may result in students not being challenged, not developing their reading prowess, or not being provided with support to meet high expectations. Text complexity matters because student learning matters.

Figure 1.6 Decision Pathways for Selecting Texts

Path 1 It's a Fantastic Text . . .	Path 2 My Students Need Reading Instruction About . . .	Path 3 I Want to Build My Students' Knowledge About . . .
What are my learning intentions?	What are my learning intentions?	What are my learning intentions?
Text Consideration: What are the qualitative and quantitative characteristics of the proposed text?	**Reader Consideration:** What are the reader's (or readers') cognitive capabilities, motivation, knowledge, and experiences?	**Reader Consideration:** What are the reader's (or readers') cognitive capabilities, motivation, knowledge, and experiences?
Reader Consideration: What are the reader's (or readers') cognitive capabilities, motivation, knowledge, and experiences?	**Text Consideration:** What are the qualitative and quantitative characteristics of the proposed text?	**Text Consideration:** What are the qualitative and quantitative characteristics of the proposed text?
Gap Analysis: What gap exists between the reader and the text I am considering?	**Gap Analysis:** What gap exists between the reader and the text I am considering?	**Gap Analysis:** What gap exists between the reader and the text I am considering?
Task Consideration: What instructional arrangement will best address this gap (teacher-led, peer-led, or independent)?	**Task Consideration:** What instructional arrangement will best address this gap (teacher-led, peer-led, or independent)?	**Task Consideration:** What instructional arrangement will best address this gap (teacher-led, peer-led, or independent)?
Text-Task Suitability: Does the proposed text align with the proposed task?	**Text-Task Suitability:** Does the proposed text align with the proposed task?	**Text-Task Suitability:** Does the proposed text align with the proposed task?
If **yes**, finalize decision and monitor progress toward identified learning intentions. If **no**, return to task consideration.	If **yes**, finalize decision and monitor progress toward learning intentions. If **no**, return to text consideration.	If **yes**, finalize decision and monitor progress toward learning intentions. If **no**, return to text and task considerations.

© Chris Hendrickson/Masterfile/Corbis

Quantitative Measures of Text Complexity

One dimension of text complexity involves quantitative measures. These primarily focus on the characteristics of the words themselves and their appearance in sentences and paragraphs. Conventional quantitative text measures do not take into account the functions of words and phrases to convey meaning, but rather focus on those elements that lend themselves to being counted, and therefore calculated. These surface structures are collectively described as readability formulas, and primarily measure semantic difficulty and sentence complexity. Gunning (2003) reports that while more than one hundred readability formulas have been developed since the 1920s, only a handful are regularly used today.

To provide a historical context for thinking about the components of readability formulas, we need to review some of the history. In 1935, Gray and Leary analyzed 228 text variables and divided them into four types: content, style, format, and organization. They could not find an easy way to measure content, format, or organization, but they could measure variables of style. From their list of seventeen variables of style, they selected five to create a formula:

1. Average sentence length
2. Number of different hard words
3. Number of personal pronouns
4. Percentage of unique words
5. Number of prepositional phrases

Their formula had a correlation of .645 with comprehension as measured by reading tests given to eight hundred adults. These criteria have been applied to varying degrees in nearly all readability formulas since their original studies.

▶ Word-Level Analysis

There is a strong foundation for using quantitative measures to determine the relative level of challenge posed to a reader. The first level of analysis is at the word level. The overall length of the word suggests the degree to which a reader must decode the word, with single-syllable words considered to be easier than multisyllabic ones. As well, the frequency with which the word appears in a language supposes its familiarity to the reader. The *Brown Corpus*, developed in 1964 by Francis and Kucera at Brown University, used computational analysis of over a million words drawn from five hundred written sources, including novels, newspapers, and scientific journals, to determine each word's degree of occurrence in American English. They determined that the words *the*, *to*, and *of* collectively comprised 13 percent of the corpus, or body of words in the language. Word frequency lists used in readability formulas may number in the thousands, or even millions, but all attempt to rank-order a word's frequency of use within specific text types. The most comprehensive review of word frequency completed to date is *The Educator's Word Frequency Guide* (Zeno, Ivens, Millard, & Duvvuri, 1995), which is a listing of printed words that has been organized by how often a particular word appears in texts encountered by students at a specific grade level.

However, word frequency alone is an incomplete measure, since the context in which the word appears can increase text complexity. In order

Conventional quantitative text measures do not take into account the functions of words and phrases to convey meaning, but rather focus on those elements that lend themselves to being counted, and therefore calculated.

to focus more specifically on school-aged readers, in the 1940s, Dale, later aided by O'Rourke, began developing a list of words that 80 percent of fourth graders would recognize and know. Over time, these evolved to a list of three thousand words (Chall & Dale, 1995). The genius of this work is that the researchers didn't just make a list; they applied this list as a way of determining the challenge readers might experience depending on the number of words *not* on the list. In other words (excuse the pun), a text with a higher percentage of words not among the three thousand could indicate a higher degree of complexity. Thus, a text with the words *field*, *meadow*, and *pasture* (which appear on the list) would not be deemed as difficult as a text that used the words *steppe* and *mead*, which do not appear on the list. The application of such a word list took into account what the reader might be expected to know, as well as the vocabulary demand of a word. Other word frequency lists developed since then build a corpus, or body, that is reflective of the use of a group of people, such as fourth graders or students entering high school. A key factor in this list is that Dale and O'Rourke tested and retested these words with students over a period of several decades and eventually published the list as *The Living Word Vocabulary* (1976). This sets it apart from other frequency lists.

▶ Sentence-Level Analysis

A second level of analysis included in nearly all quantitative readability formulas is the length of the sentence. The number of words in a sentence is a proxy for several syntactic and semantic demands on a reader (e.g., prepositional phrases, dependent clauses, adjectives, and adverbs). Taken together, these press a reader's working memory to keep a multitude of concepts and connections in mind (Kintsch, 1974). Consider the following sentence from Sandra Cisneros's short story, "Eleven," about a young girl embarrassed by the shabbiness of her sweater:

> This is when I wish I wasn't eleven, because all the years inside of me—ten, nine, eight, seven, six, five, four, three, two and one—are pushing at the back of my eyes when I put one arm through one sleeve of the sweater that smells like cottage cheese, and then the other arm through the other and stand there with my arms apart like if the sweater hurts me and it does, all itchy and full of germs that aren't even mine. (Cisneros, 1991, p. 8)

At eighty-three words, this sentence requires the reader to process several concepts simultaneously: the sweater and its smell and feel, the clause that lists a descending sequence of numbers, the use of the word *other* to refer first to the girl's arm and then to her sleeve. An analysis of individual words alone would be insufficient; all but two appear on the Dale-Chall Word List (*itchy* and *germs* do not). We deliberately selected a long sentence to illustrate a point—sentence length can be a valid indicator of the cognitive load.

Except when it's not. Very short sentences can also tax a reader:

For sale: Baby shoes, never worn.

Legend has it that this six-word story was written by Ernest Hemingway to settle a bar bet. All of the words appear on the Dale-Chall Word List. However, the level of inference and background knowledge needed to understand this text would challenge young readers. Readability formulas offer us a level of quantitative analysis that is not readily apparent, but should be augmented by the qualitative analyses that only a human reader can offer (Anderson, Hiebert, Scott, & Wilkinson, 1985).

We have taken time to discuss issues of word length, syllables, frequency of occurrence, and word lists because they are widely regarded as being proxies for the time needed for a reader to read the text, and the extent to which it taxes a reader's working memory (Just & Carpenter, 1992). As noted by Gunning (2003), these variables can be used as measures of semantic complexity. His insights echoed many of the dimensions described by Gray and Leary in 1935:

- Number of words not on a list of words tested and found to be known by most students at a certain grade level
- Number of words not on a list of high-frequency words
- Grade levels of the words
- Number of syllables in the words
- Number of letters in a word
- Number of different words in a selection
- Number of words having three or more syllables
- Frequency with which the words appear in print (p. 176)

▶ Conventional Readability Formulas

Conventional readability formulas have been utilized extensively as a means to replace outdated grade-level formulas for rating text difficulty. An advantage of these readability formulas is that teachers can easily compute them using any reading material. A few of the more common formulas, and how they are used to determine readability, are reviewed next. As a way to highlight some of the differences among these, we'll analyze a passage from *The Hunger Games* (Collins, 2008). This passage (see Figure 2.1), from about the middle of the book, contains a proper noun (a character's name, *Peeta*) and some words that have been introduced previously, such as *tributes*. According to Scholastic, overall readability or the quantifiable features of the book is 5.3 grade level, but the publisher recommends the content for students in Grades 7–8.

Individual passages within the book are harder, as we will see, which means other passages must be easier. This is an important point in considering quantitative difficulty—the law of averages is at work. That does not mean that the entire text is readable just because the average suggests it is so. That said, readability formulas can be used to guide text selection in a quick and easy way. They just aren't the only guide available to teachers.

Figure 2.1   Excerpt From *The Hunger Games*

After the anthem, the tributes file back into the Training Center lobby and onto the elevators. I make sure to veer into a car that does not contain Peeta. The crowd slows our entourages of stylists and mentors and chaperones, so we have only each other for company. No one speaks. My elevator stops to deposit four tributes before I am alone and then find the doors opening on the twelfth floor. Peeta has only just stepped from his car when I slam my palms into his chest. He loses his balance and crashes into an ugly urn with fake flowers.

Source: Collins (2008, p. 134).

Quantitative reading formulas are notoriously unreliable on works designed for beginning readers. Hiebert and Martin (2001) note that unique characteristics of the emergent reader make issues of decodability, independent word recognition, and pattern mastery more specialized than a simple measure of readability can identify. In addition, the sentence structures for these materials may be very short, sometimes a single word, with heavy reliance on illustrations from which the reader can draw extensive support. For these reasons, most quantitative readability formulas do not report expected measures for texts designed for very young children, primarily kindergarten and first grade. Poems, which by nature often use single words, phrases, fragments, and unconventional punctuation, also do not yield useful readability scores.

Fry Readability Formula

The primary appeal of the Fry readability formula is its ease of use, and the fact that it does not require any specialized software or hardware. Edward Fry (2002) designed this simple readability rating so that it can be calculated using the graph in Figure 2.2. The teacher selects three 100-word passages from the text, preferably one each from the beginning, middle, and end. Next, the teacher counts the number of sentences and syllables in each passage, then averages each of the two factors (number of syllables

Figure 2.2   Fry Readability Graph

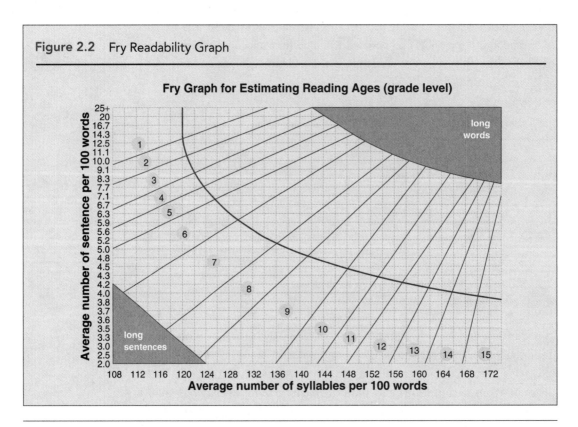

Source: Fry (2002, p. 288).

and number of sentences). These two factors are then plotted on the Fry graph to yield an approximate grade level. This readability formula does not require any computer calculations, as the algorithm is embedded in the graph. For this reason, the Fry readability formula is popular among teachers who need a quick method for gaining a sense of the approximate level of difficulty. However, it does not rely on any specific vocabulary or word frequency levels, and thus can only provide limited information about a text. Using this formula, the passage from *The Hunger Games* in Figure 2.1 scored at the seventh-grade level, which is a reasonable estimate given that the content was suggested for middle school students.

Flesch-Kincaid Grade-Level Score

Another easily accessible tool for determining readability formulas can be found on the word processing software installed on your computer. Simply type in a passage from a text you would like to assess for readability, then run the calculation. For example, the Microsoft Word® program can report a Flesch-Kincaid grade-level score to approximate difficulty, using an algorithm that includes the average sentence length (ASL) and average number of syllables per word (ASW), the same elements used to calculate the Fry readability formula: $(0.39 \times ASL) + (11.8 \times ASW) - 15.59$ (Graesser, McNamara, & Louwerse, 2011, p. 42). This measure has a high correlation with the Fry graph.

The program will also report a Flesch reading-ease score by assigning the reading a number on a 100-point scale. On this scale, the higher the score, the easier it is to read. This formula is more commonly used in business to determine the difficulty of workplace documents. Both the Flesch-Kincaid and Flesch reading-ease measures calculate using the same text characteristics, but the algorithms are weighted differently to ensure that easier texts are reported as lower numbers for the grade-level purposes, and are reported as higher numbers when considering the relative ease of the text. The Flesch reading-ease score for this paragraph was a difficult 37.4, and the Flesch-Kincaid grade-level score was 12.0. The *Hunger Games* passage in Figure 2.1 received a reading-ease score of 70.7, meaning that it could be understood by students ages thirteen to fifteen, and earned a Flesch-Kincaid grade-level score of 6.9.

Advantage-TASA Open Standard

The Advantage-TASA Open Standard, a computerized readability formula more commonly called ATOS, is used by Renaissance Learning to gauge texts used with the Accelerated Reader software. Its name reflects the partnership between Renaissance Learning (formerly Advantage Learning) and Touchstone Applied Science Associates (TASA), which developed the Degrees of Reading Power (DRP) tests. *The Educator's Word Frequency Guide* (Zeno et al., 1995) is used to determine the grade level of the words. The ATOS formula computes words per sentence, average grade level of words, and characters per word, as measured by the entire text, not just sample passages. In addition, it factors whether the text is fiction or nonfiction (the latter is considered more difficult) and the length of the book (longer texts are more difficult).

Practical advantages of the ATOS measure include the large number of trade books in its database (160,000) and the free calculation service for measuring other texts such as magazine articles and short stories. As with all readability formulas, ATOS does not take content into consideration, so *The Catcher in the Rye* (Salinger, 1951) carries a grade-level rating of 4.7. The makers caution that this measure should not be used in isolation, and each book also carries an "Interest Level" measure to further guide educators, students, and parents. Therefore, the same text has an Interest Level rating as Upper Grades (9–12). *The Hunger Games* earns a book-level measure of 5.3, but an Interest Level of Upper Middle Grades (6 and up).

▶ Readability Formulas That Also Assess Readers

Conventional readability formulas do not factor other elements that can influence difficulty, such as content. For example, a Flesch-Kincaid grade-level analysis on a hundred-word passage from *Cat's Cradle* by Kurt Vonnegut (1998), a decidedly adult satire of a world on the brink of an apocalypse, reveals a grade-level score of 2.3 because the passage contains short, clipped dialogue. While this is not a typical result, it does highlight some shortcomings when relying on readability formulas alone without considering the content or the reader. In the 1980s and 1990s, two readability formulas were developed that attempted to account for content factors, however imperfectly, and to project estimated comprehension levels of students at each grade level. In other words, these tools can be used to assess students' reading levels and to evaluate quantitative complexity.

Degrees of Reading Power

This widely used formula uses "sentence length, number of words not on an updated version of the Dale list, and average number of letters per word"

(Gunning, 2003, p. 178). A review by Graesser, McNamara, and Louwerse (2011) found that both DRP and Lexile (discussed in the following section) correlated strongly with the Flesch-Kincaid readability measure. Gunning (2003) reports that DRP (Koslin, Zeno, & Koslin, 1987) uses a variation of an older readability formula called the Bormuth. What sets the Bormuth apart is that it was the first formula to use cloze as a criterion measure. While the DRP formula is proprietary, the Bormuth formula uses average word length (AWL), average sentence length (ASL), and average number of familiar words (AFW, defined as those words that appear on the Dale-Chall list of three thousand words) as follows:

$$\text{Bormuth Readability Score} = 0.886593 - (AWL \times 0.03640) + (AFW \times 0.161911) - (ASL \times 0.21401) - (ASL \times 0.000577) - (ASL \times 0.000005)$$

An advantage of DRP is that it calculates a reader's performance with text using the same scale so that educators can match readers and books. DRP does not make readability scores of assessed texts publicly available, so we are unable to report the DRP level for the *Hunger Games* passage in Figure 2.1.

TextEvaluator

Originally developed as SourceRater as a tool to select passages for use on assessments, TextEvaluator provides a single, overall measure of text complexity using a scale that ranges from 100 (appropriate for extremely young readers) to 2,000 (appropriate for college graduates). This is similar to the scales used in other tools, including Lexile. A unique feature of TextEvaluator is that it also produces information about text variation and which of the eight factors may contribute to the complexity. Some of these factors are familiar (e.g., academic vocabulary, word unfamiliarity, syntactic complexity), but some are less so, including the following:

- **Concreteness** measures the number of words that evoke clear and meaningful mental images as they are likely to be less difficult than those that do not.
- **Lexical cohesion** measures the likelihood that the text will be seen as a "coherent message" compared with a collection of unrelated clauses and sentences.
- **Level of argumentation** measures the ease or difficulty of inferring connections across sentences when the text is argumentative.

- **Degree of narrativity** measures the features that indicate it is more characteristic of narrative than nonnarrative or expository writing.
- **Interactive/conversational style** measures the degree of conversational style.

Reading Maturity Metric

At this time, the Reading Maturity Metric is in beta testing by Pearson publishers. It's an appealing tool because it relies on word maturity, or the ways in which meanings of words and passages change as learners develop literacy skills (Landauer, Kireyev, & Panaccione, 2011). As an example, consider the word *trust*. A younger person may know the word as it relates to confidence. A person with more word maturity also knows that it can be a type of organization, often with funds associated with it. Thus the phrase *trust baby* is unclear without the context, and the Reading Maturity Metric is being tested to take into account the sophistication of a reader's word knowledge.

Lexile

This commercially available readability formula, developed by Smith, Stenner, Horabin, and Smith (1989), is used widely by textbook and trade publishers and testing companies to designate relative text difficulty among products. For example, the National Assessment of Educational Progress (NAEP) and the Programme for International Student Assessment (PISA) both use Lexile. Like DRP, the Lexile scale relies on a 2,000-point scale that is used to describe both readers and text, making it easier for teachers to match one to the other. The Lexile scale score assigned to *The Hunger Games* is 810, which means that it would be of appropriate reading difficulty for students in fourth or fifth grade. As we have noted, however, many of the themes in the book are not appropriate for students at this grade level.

Each of the tools we have discussed has aligned with grade-level equivalents, and each provides a range for reading proficiency, not a specific and exact target that must be met.

Both DRP and the Lexile scale rely on conventional text analysis algorithms, with one notable exception: they can be used to assess students in order to pair texts with readers. Both measures apply a similar approach to assessing students, using cloze items within reading passages. By using the same scale, a teacher can match a student's DRP or Lexile scale score with a text at that same level. Additionally, teachers can use information about a reader's quantitative score to identify texts that appropriately challenge him or her.

The readability formulas discussed in this chapter thus far vary somewhat in their algorithms and the factors they use to quantify a text. These formulas draw on characteristics that serve as approximations of overall difficulty: length of word, frequency of occurrence in the language, number of syllables, sentence length, or inclusion of words on a specific word list, such as the Dale-Chall list. Some of these formulas are better than others at predicting comprehension. We present a number of different formulas because each is used, to a varying degree, in school systems, and thus informed practitioners should understand what the formula is measuring and what it is not measuring. That said, most of the formulas account for about 50 percent of the variation in comprehension. The Lexile formula is better, predicting about 75 percent of the variation (see Smith, Stenner, Horabin, & Smith, 1989).

Each of the tools we have discussed thus far has aligned with grade-level equivalents (see Figure 2.3). Note that there is overlap across the grades, meaning that the upper end of one grade will likely not begin the next grade. Each tool provides a range for reading proficiency, not a specific and exact target that must be met.

Figure 2.3 Common Scale for Band Level Text Difficulty Ranges

Common Scale for Band	Text Analyzer Tools					
	ATOS	DRP	FK	Lexile	RM	SR
2nd–3rd	2.75–5.14	42–54	1.98–5.34	420–820	3.53–6.13	0.05–2.48
4th–5th	4.97–7.03	52–60	4.51–7.73	740–1010	5.42–7.92	0.84–5.75
6th–8th	7.00–9.98	57–67	6.51–10.34	925–1185	7.04–9.57	4.11–10.66
9th–10th	9.67–12.01	62–72	8.32–12.12	1050–1335	8.41–10.81	9.02–13.93
11th–CCR	11.20–14.10	67–74	10.34–14.20	1185–1385	9.57–12.00	12.30–14.50

Source: National Governors Association & Council of Chief State School Officers (n.d.).

Key:

ATOS = ATOS® (Renaissance Learning)

DRP = Degrees of Reading Power® (Questar Assessment, Inc.)

FK = Flesch Kincaid® (public domain, no mass analyzer tool available)

Lexile = Lexile Framework® (MetaMetrics)

RM = Pearson Reading Maturity Metric© (Pearson Education)

SR = SourceRater© (Educational Testing Service)

Measures not in concordance table:

REAP (Carnegie Mellon University)

Coh-Metrix (University of Memphis)

▶ Measuring Coreference and Cohesion

One concern raised by some educators and reading researchers is that coherence and cohesion primarily measure surface-level complexity but do not get at deeper levels of meaning that are necessary to read longer and more sophisticated texts (Davison & Kantor, 1982). A newer readability measure, called Coh-Metrix, attempts to look at the deeper structures of a text, especially in its ability to present ideas coherently. These analyses have primarily been within the fields of linguistics, artificial intelligence, and computational linguistics (Graesser, McNamara, & Louwerse, 2011). With the advancement of newer tools of analysis, especially those that can parse texts at a fine-grained level and those that account for cohesion (the relationship between given and new knowledge), a more complex method of computing readability includes aspects of both semantic and syntactic features.

One such tool, latent semantic analysis (LSA), which Coh-Metrix uses, offers a way to move beyond surface-level measures of word and sentence length and word frequency, to mathematically measure how words and phrases connect with other words and phrases across a text (Landauer, McNamara, Dennis, & Kinstch, 2007). This measure also takes into account the amount of implicit knowledge needed to understand the relationships between words and ideas. For instance, the word *cup* is associated with other words such as *fork* and *plate*, as well as *coffee*, *set the table*, and *wash the dishes*, even though these terms may not appear in the text. An LSA analysis forms a map, or matrix, of connections that are beyond a human's ability to detect and measure.

In addition to LSA measures, computational linguistics researchers have sought to further quantify other elements of text, including parts of speech, genre of the text, psycholinguistic dimensions of words such as relative level of abstraction or concreteness, and propositional density (how a noun phrase is linked to an agent, recipient, location, or object). These and other related measures work together to influence a text's *coreference* (the extent to which a word or phrase references similar words or phrases in the surrounding text). For instance, argument overlap "is the most robust measure of lexical coreferentiality in that it measures how often two sentences share common arguments (nouns, pronouns, and noun phrases)" (Crossley, Dufty, McCarthy, & McNamara, 2007, p. 199). As a simple example, consider these two sentences:

The bookshelves sagged under the weight of the heavy, dusty books. No one had checked out these books from the library for many years, as evidenced by the infrequent checkout dates on the cards in their lonely front pockets.

The word *library* locates the bookshelves and the books, and the word *their* coreferences *books* in both the first and second sentences. *Checked out* and *checkout* are different parts of speech, but they coreference each other due to proximity as well as agency. A latent semantic analysis of the same short passage might reveal that there are further relationships beyond the text, including *librarian*, *library card*, and the process needed to borrow and return a book. Taken together, latent semantic analysis, psycholinguistic measures, and coreferencing combine to contribute to a text's cohesion—that is, the number of its meaning relations. We are speaking not of the overarching meanings related to theme, main ideas, and so on, but rather of the way syntax and semantics interact to develop a coherent message within and across sentences and paragraphs within the same text. This tool uses sixty-four indices that report on measures, or metrics, related to the research on discourse, language, and cognition to assign text difficulty.

The Coh-Metrix tool is available at no cost at http://cohmetrix.com. Perhaps the most valuable application of Coh-Metrix is in the authors' recommendations about the identification of texts across five dimensions, each addressing a specific purpose and reader:

1. **Challenging Texts With Associated Explanations.** Some assigned texts are considerably beyond students' ability level. In such cases, students need comments by a teacher, tutor, group, or computer that explain technical vocabulary and points of difficulty. Students are greatly stretched by exposure to difficult content, strategies, and associated explanations.

2. **Texts at the Zone of Proximal Development.** Some assigned texts are slightly above the difficulty level that students can handle. These texts gently push the envelope—they are not too easy or too difficult, but just right.

3. **Easy Texts to Build Self-Efficacy.** Easy texts are assigned to build reading fluency and self-efficacy. Struggling readers can lose

self-confidence, self-efficacy, and motivation when beset with a high density of texts that they can barely handle, if at all.

4. **A Balanced Diet of Texts at Varying Difficulty.** Texts may be assigned according to a distribution of alternatives 1, 2, and 3 above, mostly in the zone of proximal development. The balanced diet benefits from exposure to challenging texts, texts that gradually push the envelope, and texts that build self-efficacy. This approach also includes texts in different genres.

5. **Texts Tailored to Develop Particular Reading Components.** Texts may be assigned adaptively in a manner that is sensitive to the student's complex profile of reading components. The texts attempt to rectify particular reading deficits or to advance particular reading skills. (Graesser, McNamara, & Kulikowich, 2011, p. 232)

These recommendations challenge us to apply quantitative measures in ways that create a text gradient that not only considers the reading itself but also takes the reader and the learning context into account. This, however, has not been seen as the primary function of quantitative reading formulas, and their use and misuse has resulted in cautions and criticisms.

▶ Cautions About Quantitative Analysis of Text

As we have noted, quantitative measures used in isolation can result in inappropriate content being assigned to students. That doesn't mean that these tools and their resulting data are useless; rather, they have to be interpreted and used in conjunction with qualitative factors of text complexity. It is misguided and problematic to demand that teachers use texts that fall only within the quantitative text range associated with a specific tool. Text selection is multidimensional, not unidimensional. Further, selecting texts based only on the quantitative score is a form of censorship, blocking students from information and ideas that they may want to explore, simply because of the words and sentence structures the author used.

Another criticism of quantitative reading formulas is that they have been used as a device to manipulate text to meet a fixed numerical value, regardless of its effect on the text itself. For example, publishers may remove or substitute words or phrases in order to lower the quantitative score, but in the process inadvertently make the reading more difficult to understand. For example, signal words such as *first* and *last*, and transitional phrases like *in conclusion*, add length to the sentence and can thereby raise the score. But words like these actually assist the reader by helping him or her internally organize the information. In fact, from a qualitative perspective (discussed further in Chapters 3 and 4), a profusion of signal words alerts the teacher to the fact that a text is using an internal structure to scaffold the reader's understanding. Conversely, their removal can lower the readability score but end up making the text far less coherent. Higher readability scores do not automatically signal difficulty. Beck, McKeown, Omanson, and Pople (1984) demonstrated that texts with higher levels of coherence and vocabulary were easier to comprehend than similar texts that had been stripped of these features.

Selecting texts based only on the quantitative score is a form of censorship, blocking students from information and ideas that they may want to explore, simply because of the words and sentence structures the author used.

Informational texts that use a high degree of technical vocabulary may score much higher due to the relative rarity in the general corpus, with no way to account for their much more frequent use in a specific text. For example, science texts have technical vocabulary that is comparatively rare on word frequency lists but is commonly used within a discipline (Cohen & Steinberg, 1983). The word *photosynthesis* is rare when compared to all words, but much more frequent in the field of life sciences. Therefore, a biology textbook might have a higher readability score due to the presence of such a word, despite the fact that the topic is deeply explored within its pages. *The Educator's Word Frequency Guide* (Zeno et al., 1995) was developed in part to address these discipline-specific concerns, and provides an "index of dispersion" for the use of such words.

▶ Conclusion

Since the early part of the 20th century, educators have sought ways to order or level text through quantitative measures of readability. These formulas vary somewhat, but primarily measure surface-level features of a text, especially focusing on word and sentence length and frequency of word occurrence on a generated list. More recent developments utilize the availability of digitized texts to analyze longer texts, not just samples. Most important, advances in computational linguistics, psychology, and artificial intelligence have opened the door to a new generation of analytic tools that provide a more fine-grained measure of the relationships of words to one another and the mental models that are necessary to understand them. A summary of the readability formulas discussed in this chapter can be found in Figure 2.4.

As with all measures, each can report accurately on some aspects, while other equally important elements remain untouched. For this reason, quantitative measures should be viewed as an important step, but by no means a final one or necessarily the first one, in determining the optimum text for a reader. Readability, after all, should never be confused with reading ability. In the next chapters, we explore another necessary element for determining text complexity: qualitative analysis of literary and informational texts.

Figure 2.4 Summary of Quantitative Text Measures

Name	Purpose	Factors Used	Ease of Use	Notes
Fry Readability Formula	Assesses text difficulty	Sentence length and syllables	Easy; use graph	Primary–college
Flesch-Kincaid Grade-Level Score	Assesses text difficulty	Sentence length and syllables	Easy; use word processing software	K–12
Flesch Reading-Ease Score	Assesses text difficulty	Sentence length and syllables	Easy; use word processing software	Reports relative ease as compared to students in Grade 5–college
Advantage-TASA Open Standard (ATOS)	Assesses text difficulty	Words per sentence, grade level of words, and character length across entire text	Easy; free online calculator and extensive published booklist	Factors fiction/nonfiction and length of text
Degrees of Reading Power (DRP)	Assesses text difficulty and reader skills using same scale	Sentence length and relative word frequency	Hard; proprietary software	Designed as criterion-referenced measures for use in Grades 1–12
TextEvaluator	Assesses text difficulty and identifies problematic areas	Vocabulary and sentence structures	Hard; uploaded text must meet all requirements	Considers a range of factors that impact comprehension
Lexile Scale	Assesses text difficulty and reader skills using same scale	Sentence length and relative word frequency	Hard; proprietary software Easy; searchable database	Reports as grade bands (Grades 2+), uses a similar scale to report student reading ability as measured by cloze items
Coh-Metrix	Assesses texts on 64 indices, including measures of text cohesion, linguistic elements, and parsers	Parsers, propositions, and latent semantic analysis, as well as traditional readability measures	Easy; use online calculator	Reports require a high degree of technical knowledge to interpret

© John Van Hasselt/Corbis

Qualitative Values of Literary Texts

*B*ug is a fairly easy word. Most students have background knowledge about bugs and know the label for the concept of bug. The word itself would not cause readers much trouble, and readability formulas would not indicate that this was an especially difficult word. But consider how the word is used in the following sentences.

When I saw the bug, I screamed for help.

When I saw the bug, I remembered my first car.

When I saw the bug, I wondered who was spying on me.

Sometimes there are words or phrases that throw off the reader yet are not picked up by readability formulas. While this is a simple example, it helps us make a point: it takes a human to notice these aspects of text. As Bailin and Grafstein (2001) noted, readability formulas are

> both seductive and misleading: seductive, because the application of a mathematical formula lends an aura of scientific objectivity to the number derived from it, and misleading, because the apparent objectivity of the score lulls naïve educators or librarians into having greater confidence in it than they would in their own informal judgments, and certainly more than is warranted by the evidence. (p. 8)

We agree that readability formulas are seductive and can be misleading when used without attention to qualitative values, as well as reader and task characteristics. When we look at a large number of texts, readability formulas can help us initially narrow the range of selections a teacher might be considering. But quantitative measures of readability are not very good at things a human reader needs to notice. The president of MetaMetrics, the company that produces the Lexile, noted this in an interview:

> While a Lexile measure is a valuable piece of information in the book-selection process, it's important to note that the Lexile measure is only one piece of information to consider when selecting a book for a specific student. Other factors, such as the content and quality of the text, and the student's interests and reading goals, should also be considered. (Harvey, 2011, p. 58)

In other words, we need to look beyond readability to understand the nature of the text under consideration. There are three overlapping qualitative features of any text that contribute to a reader's ability to comprehend it: structure, coherence, and audience appropriateness (e.g., Boscolo & Mason, 2003; Kobayashi, 2002; Meyer, 2003). In this chapter, we discuss the properties of literary texts, in contrast to informational text types, which are addressed in the following chapter. From there, we focus on qualitative values of literary texts, which in turn provide insight into understanding what needs to be taught, and in what manner.

▶ Characteristics of Literary Texts

From the time we are infants, we humans surround ourselves with narrative in both oral and written forms. We tell each other stories to recount events, to transmit information. A narrative can serve many purposes, from entertaining, to inspiring, and even to serving as the conduit for a much-needed call to action. Above all else, narrative texts convey an experience, whether real or imagined.

Readability formulas are seductive and can be misleading when used without attention to qualitative values, as well as reader and task characteristics.

Most narratives take a *literary* form, often that of a novel, short story, biography or autobiography, poem, or song. However, despite the fact that they typically take on these somewhat predictable forms, literary narratives are sometimes incorrectly cataloged and categorized across a fiction/nonfiction divide. This confusion is due, in part, to the fact that narrative text types are often embedded in readings that are otherwise informational. Think of an article you recently read that included an illustrative experience that made the information come alive. Contemporary nonfiction writers like Malcolm Gladwell, Elizabeth Gilbert, Atul Gawande, and Peggy Orenstein intersperse their largely informational writing with stories that make their arguments understandable. As well, many of the nonfiction titles read by children and adolescents have a substantial narrative component.

Literary texts that employ a narrative form have characters, and writers use direct and indirect characterization techniques to help readers understand the interior and exterior lives of the characters. These characterization techniques include descriptions of a character's appearance, but his or her attitudes and beliefs are also revealed more subtly through actions, dialogue, and the reactions of other characters. Dialogue can pose a special challenge for young readers, especially as markers are less frequently used to track who is speaking (e.g., "said Kendra") as texts become more developmentally complex. As well, writers infuse dialogue with hidden meaning. Consider this conversation between two characters in Hemingway's "Hills

Like White Elephants" (1927/1998, p. 211) who are looking at a mountain range in the distance:

> "They look like white elephants," she says.
> "I've never seen one," the man says, and drinks his beer.
> "No, you wouldn't have."
> "I might have," the man says. "Just because you say I wouldn't have doesn't prove anything."

Even without knowing anything else about the story, you can surmise that the characters are a couple, and they are sniping at one another. The author, a master of dialogue, never says so, and yet experienced readers are able to locate the subtext.

Literary texts employing a narrative form have plot-driven structures. This is initially taught to primary students as story grammar, which includes characters, setting, problem, and solution. As readers mature, they learn to analyze elements of plot structure as outlined by Freytag (see Figure 3.1), including exposition (introduction to the theme, setting, characters, and circumstances), rising action, climax, falling action, and resolution. We believe it is also important to consider issues of conflict, which others might include as circumstances or rising action. When a literary text does not follow this convention, as is the case in "An Upheaval" by Chekhov (1917/2012), in which the exposition occurs throughout the short story and there is no resolution, readers have a harder time understanding it.

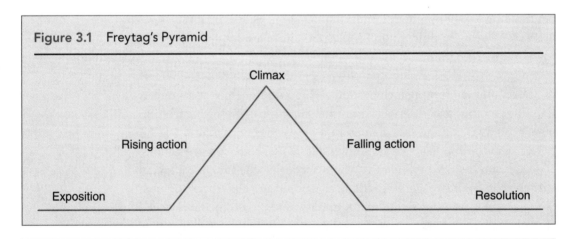

Figure 3.1 Freytag's Pyramid

Climax

Rising action

Falling action

Exposition

Resolution

Source: Adapted from Freytag (1863).

Literary texts can also use expository text structures. For example, *There Was an Old Lady Who Swallowed a Fly* (Taback, 1997) is a narrative for young children told as a sequence story. Understanding that it is fiction, has a plot structure, and is told in a backward chronological order helps kindergarten students make meaning of the text.

Some literary texts make extensive use of informational structures, which in turn can strain a reader's comprehension and fluency. The structure used by Steinbeck in *The Grapes of Wrath* (1939/2006) reflects the book's origins in a newspaper series, and the chapters present a straightforward narrative of the Joad family interspersed with reports of banking practices, tenant farming, and government camps. As high school teachers can attest, the variation in text types is challenging for readers who are accustomed to a continuous narrative that progresses chronologically.

▶ Specialized Literary Texts

There is a subset of literary texts that, due to their brevity, cannot be validly measured with the use of quantitative methods of analysis. As we noted in the previous chapter, there are texts designed for very young readers and used during guided reading (often called "leveled" books) that are of such short length that they may have sentences of only one or two words. But note the similarity that these types of texts share with poems and song lyrics. They, too, use short phrases and sentences that are laden with meaning. In the case of many poems, the graphic layout of the words on the page also conveys meaning. These graphic elements may be over-whelmingly apparent, as in concrete poems that are intentionally laid out in a recognizable shape. At other times, the effect is more subtle, as when e. e. cummings manipulates syntax, punctuation, and spacing conventions. Therefore, these specialized literary texts can be evaluated only by using a qualitative scale.

▶ Analyzing Literary Texts Qualitatively

The plot-driven nature of many literary texts and the presence of characters who are flat or round (meaning they either remain static or undergo change and development throughout the story) are just two examples of narrative elements that play into the qualitative analysis of a given text. Other considerations relevant to this analysis include the use of imagery and point of view. Beyond this, there are other qualitative factors that impact the understanding of literary texts. Standards documents organize these elements across four major categories: levels of meanings and purpose, structure, language conventionality and clarity, and knowledge demands. These factors should be used to further identify texts, teaching points, and tasks.

A scale for qualitatively analyzing literary texts can be found in Figure 3.2, and will serve as a means for organizing the remainder of the chapter. Keep in mind that the purpose is not to rank texts in isolation of readers and the tasks they will engage in. Task–text suitability for the reader is paramount. Rather, this scale should be used as one step in your decision pathway, whether you have located a text you would like to use (Path 1), are looking for a text to use for reading instruction (Path 2), or are seeking a text for content and background knowledge purposes (Path 3).

Use this scale for a quick assessment of a reader–text relationship that results in an end score ranging from 3 (*stretch*) to 1 (*comfortable*). Scoring the reader–text relationship provides a composite overview of the areas in which further instruction is needed and further informs your decisions about the task (whether teacher-led, collaborative, or independent). For example, when several ninth graders wanted to form a book club to read *I Am Nujood, Age 10 and Divorced* (Ali & Minoui, 2010), their teacher used this scale. She discovered that the only areas in which the reader–text relationship would receive a score of 3 were in the subcategories identified within the major section of knowledge demands. Further analysis of the subcategories helped the teacher to craft an initial instructional conversation with this group that involved discussing the location, history, customs, religion, and cultural beliefs in Yemen and the Middle East regarding the marriage of young girls. Armed with this foundational knowledge, these students were then able to participate in their book club and later create a shared blog, which included drawings and photos illustrating their interpretations of the courage they felt was shown by Nujood through her story of defiance.

Similarly, when a third-grade teacher evaluated *Throw Your Tooth on the Roof: Tooth Traditions From Around the World* (Beeler, 1998), a nonfiction text with substantial narrative passages, she determined that while the quantitative reading measure would be accessible for most of her students, other factors contributed to its complexity. The diverse geographic locations and unfamiliar cultures made the text more demanding in regard to background

Figure 3.2 Qualitative Scale of Literary Texts

Score	3 points (Stretch) Texts That Would Stretch a Reader and/or Require Instruction	2 points (Grade Level) Texts That Require Grade-Appropriate Skills	1 point (Comfortable) Texts That Are Comfortable and/or Build Background, Fluency, and Skills
Levels of Meaning and Purpose			
Density and Complexity	Significant density and complexity, with multiple levels of meaning; meanings may be more ambiguous	Single, but more complex or abstract level of meaning; some meanings are stated, while others are left to the reader to identify	Single and literal levels of meaning; meaning is explicitly stated
Figurative Language	Figurative language plays a significant role in identifying the meaning of the text; more sophisticated figurative language is used (irony and satire, allusions, archaic or less familiar symbolism); the reader is left to interpret these meanings	Figurative language such as imagery, metaphors, symbolism, and personification is used to make connections within the text to more explicit information, and readers are supported in understanding these language devices through examples and explanations	Limited use of symbolism, metaphors, and poetic language that allude to other unstated concepts; language is explicit and relies on literal interpretations
Purpose	Purpose is deliberately withheld from the reader, who must use other interpretative skills to identify it	Purpose is implied but is easily identified based on title or context	Purpose or main idea is directly and explicitly stated at the beginning of the reading
Structure			
Genre	Genre is unfamiliar or bends and expands the rules for the genre	Genre is either unfamiliar but a reasonable example of it or a familiar genre that bends and expands the rules for the genre	Genre is familiar, and the text is consistent with the elements of that genre

(Continued)

Figure 3.2 (Continued)

Score	3 points (Stretch) Texts That Would Stretch a Reader and/or Require Instruction	2 points (Grade Level) Texts That Require Grade-Appropriate Skills	1 point (Comfortable) Texts That Are Comfortable and/or Build Background, Fluency, and Skills
Organization	Organization distorts time or sequence in a deliberate effort to delay the reader's full understanding of the plot, process, or set of concepts; may include significant flashbacks, foreshadowing, or shifting perspectives	Organization adheres to most conventions, but digresses on occasion to temporarily shift the reader's focus to another point of view, event, time, or place, before returning to the main idea or topic	Organization is conventional, sequential, or chronological, with clear signals and transitions to lead the reader through a story, process, or set of concepts
Narration	Unreliable narrator provides a distorted or limited view to the reader; the reader must use other clues to deduce the truth; multiple narrators provide conflicting information; shifting points of view keep the reader guessing	Third-person limited or first-person narration provides accurate, but limited, perspectives or viewpoints	Third-person omniscient narration or an authoritative and credible voice provides an appropriate level of detail and keeps little hidden from the view of the reader
Text Features and Graphics	Limited use of text features to organize information and guide the reader; information in the graphics is not repeated in the main part of the text, but is essential for understanding the text	Wider array of text features includes margin notes, diagrams, graphs, font changes, and other devices that compete for the reader's attention; graphics and visuals are used to augment and illustrate information in the main part of the text	Text features (e.g., bold and italicized words, headings and subheadings) organize information explicitly and guide the reader; graphics or illustrations may be present but are not necessary to understand the main part of the text
Language Conventionality and Clarity			
Standard English and Variations	The text includes significant and multiple styles of English and its variations, and these are unfamiliar to the reader	Some distance exists between the reader's linguistic base and the language conventions used in the text; the vernacular used is unfamiliar to the reader	Language closely adheres to the reader's linguistic base

Score	3 points (Stretch) Texts That Would Stretch a Reader and/or Require Instruction	2 points (Grade Level) Texts That Require Grade-Appropriate Skills	1 point (Comfortable) Texts That Are Comfortable and/or Build Background, Fluency, and Skills
Register	Archaic, formal, domain-specific, or scholarly register	Register is consultative or formal, and may be academic but acknowledges the developmental level of the reader	Register is casual and familiar
Knowledge Demands			
Background Knowledge	The text places demands on the reader that extend far beyond one's experiences, and provides little in the way of explanation of these divergent experiences	There is distance between the reader's experiences and those in the text, but there is acknowledgment of these divergent experiences, and sufficient explanation to bridge these gaps	The text contains content that closely matches the reader's life experiences
Prior Knowledge	Specialized or technical content knowledge is presumed, and little in the way of review or explanation of these concepts is present in the text	Subject-specific knowledge is required, but the text augments this with review or summary of this information	Prior knowledge needed to understand the text is familiar, and draws on a solid foundation of practical, general, and academic learning
Cultural Knowledge	Text relies on extensive or unfamiliar intertextuality, and uses artifacts and symbols that reference archaic or historical cultures	Text primarily references contemporary and popular culture to anchor explanations for new knowledge; intertextuality is used more extensively but is mostly familiar to the reader	The reader uses familiar cultural templates to understand the text; limited or familiar intertextuality
Vocabulary Knowledge	Vocabulary demand is extensive, domain-specific, and representative of complex ideas; the text offers little in the way of context clues to support the reader	Vocabulary draws on domain-specific, general academic, and multiple-meaning words, with text supports to guide the reader's correct interpretations of their meanings; the vocabulary used represents familiar concepts and ideas	Vocabulary is controlled and uses the most commonly held meanings; multiple-meaning words are used in a limited fashion

knowledge and cultural knowledge. As well, the overall organization of the book was comparative, with discussions of how the loss of a deciduous tooth is addressed in many societies. Based on her assessment, the teacher provided additional instruction as needed on unfamiliar cultures and locations. Importantly, she assisted her students in understanding the meta-organizational structure of the text by creating a class chart divided into continents. As they read about tooth traditions in Mexico, Cameroon, and Russia, the class composed notes on stickies about each, then consulted an atlas to determine the correct continent. This codeveloped chart provided the teacher with a tool to help students find similarities and differences within regions and to explore the broader comparisons that were implied but not explicitly stated in the book.

We do not intend for this scale to be used as if it were scientifically calibrated, because the reader—not the text in isolation—is the variable. Rather, we share it as we use it, for a quick check that helps us to assess the reader–text relationship. A stretch text for one reader is not necessarily a stretch for another. But knowing this gives us more information to inform our planning. As always, instruction should be designed to support the student's reading of the targeted text through meaningful tasks.

▶ Levels of Meaning and Purpose

Some literary texts can be taken at face value while others are more like onions, with layer upon layer of meaning. A literal reading of *Animal Farm* (Orwell, 1946), in which animals take over the farm and begin to rule themselves, is very different from a reading in which the reader understands the metaphors being used to describe Russia. For example, the Battle of the Cowshed is a metaphor for the overthrow of the old Russian government based on czars. The same range of levels of meaning can be found in picture books, chapter books, and trade books. For example, in *Cat and Mouse* (Bogacki, 1996), the literal story focuses on a cat family and a mouse family and how they become friends. But the deeper meaning focuses on what children are taught and how they can develop friendships with people who are different from them. Similarly, *Petey* (Mikaelsen, 1998) is literally about a person with a disability who lived in an institution, but there are layers of meaning related to the way that society treats people with disabilities and what it means to have friends and advocate on behalf of those friends.

Density and Complexity

In some cases, the text is dense and complex, whereas in other cases, it is literal and explicit. Straightforward texts that provide rich descriptions are less complex than those that are ambiguous or require extensive inferences. That's not to say that direct and straightforward texts are better than those that require more effort to make meaning. However, some texts challenge readers more than others to interpret meaning. Returning to *Animal Farm*, in the "Beasts of England" song, Orwell does not come right out and say that animals are going to be free from the harnesses and restraints of the government. Instead, students must recognize that the song has a Marxist tone, and that while the ideals of the rebellion are initially straightforward, they will soon be discarded as a dictatorship emerges. The following excerpt from the song takes some work to understand because the layers of meaning are complex and the author does not explicitly state that this event marks a new level of empowerment. Readers need to analyze the meaning of the anthem, and why it is a turning point in the novel.

Soon and late the day is coming,

Tyrant Man shall be o'erthrown,

And the fruitful fields of England

Shall be trod by beasts alone.

Rings shall vanish from our noses,

And the harness from our back,

Bit and spur shall rust forever,

Cruel whips no more shall crack.

Instructionally, the implications are clear. Once identified as a place in the novel where readers are likely to rush past because they don't understand its significance, the teacher can determine what tasks might need to occur. There may be further instruction on its link to the Stalinist government, or on its symbolism as a rallying point and its effect of building camaraderie among the animals. Perhaps, as suggested by Gulbin (1966), the teacher could link the similar effects of the anthem to the conch in *Lord of the Flies* (Golding, 1959).

Figurative Language

In addition to density and complexity, figurative language can make a text more complex. When authors use irony, idioms, metaphor, symbolism, or other literary devices, the reader has to think a little more. When these are not used, the text is easier to understand.

Consider the work of Dr. Seuss. He used symbolism often, which made his books harder than they might otherwise seem to be. For example, Dr. Seuss reflected on fascism in *Yertle the Turtle and Other Stories* (1958), friendship and otherness in *The Sneetches and Other Stories* (1961), environmentalism in *The Lorax* (1971), and commercialism in *How the Grinch Stole Christmas* (1957). Figurative language is not reserved for complex poetry—rather, it is all around us. When we understand figurative language, it makes the reading more interesting because our minds get a chance to work. That having been said, when we miss the figurative language, we miss a lot of the meaning of the text. If the reader does not think deeply about the metaphorical connection between a stage and life itself, for instance, he or she is not likely to understand this passage from Shakespeare's *As You Like It* (1599/1997):

> All the world's a stage,
>
> And all the men and women merely players;
>
> They have their exits and their entrances,
>
> And one man in his time plays many parts. (Act II, Scene 7, Lines 142–145)

The literary devices used by writers convey the meaning of a text, and without instruction, they are not going to be readily apparent to a young reader. A list of common literary devices can be found in Figure 3.3.

Figure 3.3 Common Literary Devices

Allegory	A story that is used to teach something (e.g., parables in the Bible, Aesop's fables); the stories are usually long and require analysis to find the allegory or intention
Alliteration	Occurs when the author uses the same letter or sound to start each word in a string (e.g., "Andrea anxiously awaited arrangement"); used frequently in books for emergent readers in part to foster phonemic awareness
Allusion	A reference to a well-known person, myth, historical event, or biblical story (e.g., "she's just like Narcissus," "it's as bad as the sinking of the *Titanic*")

Flashback	Pauses the action to comment on or portray a scene that took place earlier (e.g., during a scene in which a person walks through a dark alley, the author pauses to relate a story about another time when the character was scared)
Foreshadowing	A hint of things to come—usually, but not always, an unpleasant event
Hyperbole	An exaggerated comment or line used for effect and not meant to be taken literally (e.g., "when faced with a long line at the Department of Motor Vehicles, Andrew said, 'It will take an eternity to be allowed to drive'")
Imagery	Involves language that evokes one or all of the five senses: sight, hearing, taste, smell, and/or touching (e.g., "her lips taste of honey and dew," "walking through the halls, amid the crashing sound of lockers closing and the smell of yesterday's coffee, I saw the radiant teacher")
Irony and Satire	Use of sophisticated humor to relay a message, often saying what something is when the opposite or reverse could be true; irony used to say one thing when the author means another (e.g., "looking at the shark bite in his surfboard, James says, 'Finally, I've got a short board'"); satire used to focus more on mockery or wit to attack or ridicule something
Metaphor	Makes a direct comparison without using *like* or *as*; simply makes a comparison in which one thing is said to be another (e.g., "the dog's fur was electric, standing on end in fear")
Personification	When authors give animals, ideas, or actions the qualities of humans; common in Disney films and children's books; also used for more abstract ideas (e.g., "hate has you trapped in her arms")
Point of View	First person: story told from the perspective of the narrator, and the reader cannot know or witness anything that the narrator does not tell; second person: narrator speaks directly to the reader (e.g., "you will likely know by now that Andre is a bad guy"); third person: narrator is omniscient (all-knowing) and can convey different perspectives at different times
Simile	A comparison using *like* or *as* (e.g., "like a rain-filled cloud, Anna cried and cried when she learned of her lost fortune")
Symbolism	An object or action that means something more than its literal meaning (e.g., a black crow in the text prepares readers for death; the sighting of a white dove conveys peace or life)
Tone and Mood	The attitude an author takes toward a subject or character (e.g., hateful, serious, humorous, sarcastic, solemn, objective) through the use of dialogue, settings, or descriptions

Note: The use and understanding of literary devices allows students to understand texts and share conversations with their peers about texts using common terms. Further, as students understand increasingly complex literary devices and read them in texts, they will begin to use these devices in their writing, thus making their writing come alive.

Source: Fisher, Frey, & Lapp (2008a).

Purpose

Qualitatively speaking, the purpose of a given text also has an impact on its complexity. Some texts have subtle purposes while others have explicitly stated purposes. Sometimes the author states the purpose right up front, and other times the reader is left to figure out why the author wrote the specific text and what the author wanted the reader to know or do with the information. The role that purpose plays in determining text complexity can be easily illustrated: compare a textbook that starts each section with a clear purpose and main idea statement to a fable such as "The Boy Who Cried Wolf," in which the purpose has to be inferred. It is only at the end of this fable, when the moral of the story is understood, that the purpose becomes clear to the reader.

Again, we are not suggesting that having a clear purpose is a bad thing. When we want students to read and understand a textbook focused on U.S. history, for instance, it helps when they know the purpose. It's also important to recognize that not all texts have a clearly stated purpose, to openly acknowledge the complexity of those texts, and to teach students how to read them. Literary texts that use humor or are satirical pose a challenge to students who read and interpret meaning at the literal level. Popular novels like *Sense and Sensibility and Sea Monsters* (Austen & Winters, 2009), a takeoff on Jane Austen's comedy of manners, lose their absurdist appeal if read as serious offerings. However, the humor that comes to the fore when reading this particular novel is enhanced when the reader has read the original and can appreciate the cleverness of Ben Winters's contributions. Mark Twain's novel *A Connecticut Yankee in King Arthur's Court* (1889/2001) similarly winks at the effects of technology on a naïve citizenry, while also criticizing romantic notions of chivalry popular in the literature of the time. In fact, almost anything written by Twain is made more complex because his use of humor and satire moves the narrative from literal to interpretive.

▶ Structure

All writers use text structures to convey their ideas. As with other factors that make texts complex, these structures are sometimes simple and explicit and other times complex and implicit. Again, there is no value judgment placed on the text itself in terms of how these structures are used.

Simple and explicit is not necessarily better than complex and implicit. Rather, understanding what makes a text complex and figuring out how to help students access it must be among our primary goals as educators.

Genre

Readers should recognize the genre of the text. Although there are debates about what really constitutes a genre, most people agree that literary texts that are in the same genre have similarities in form and style. At the global level, readers should know if they are reading fiction or nonfiction. From there, they should recognize genres of texts, such as those found in Figure 3.4 on the next page. Some literary genres are unfamiliar and need to be explicitly taught—poetry comes to mind as a common example. But another genre to consider is that of the graphic novel, in which text and images are intertwined to tell a complicated narrative. The *Bone* series of graphic novels is aimed at a young audience, but its more than one thousand pages arch over a series of adventures to rival the *Lord of the Rings* trilogy. This genre requires a specialized kind of reading, in which it becomes apparent that meaning is conveyed through movement, color, the placement of graphics on the page, and the written text itself. Like many of the literary texts cited in this chapter, multiple qualitative factors are at play here—in this case, levels of meaning (*Bone* follows the heroic cycle) and visual elements, as well as genre.

Organization

Additionally, a text should be assessed qualitatively for its organization. If the organization is conventional, with a predictable flow of events, then the text is likely to be easier for students to understand. Generally, texts organized in chronological order are less complex than those that use some other organizational pattern. Many literary texts use flashbacks and foreshadowing, making the text harder to comprehend because of shifts in time. When an author violates our understanding of chronology, we have to work harder to make sense of the text at hand. This is also the case with texts that have generally unconventional organizational patterns, such as *Voices in the Park* (Browne, 1998), in which each section features a different voice (character) recounting the same event. The font also changes with each character—a subtle difference for young readers—making the text harder to understand.

Figure 3.4   Genre Wheel

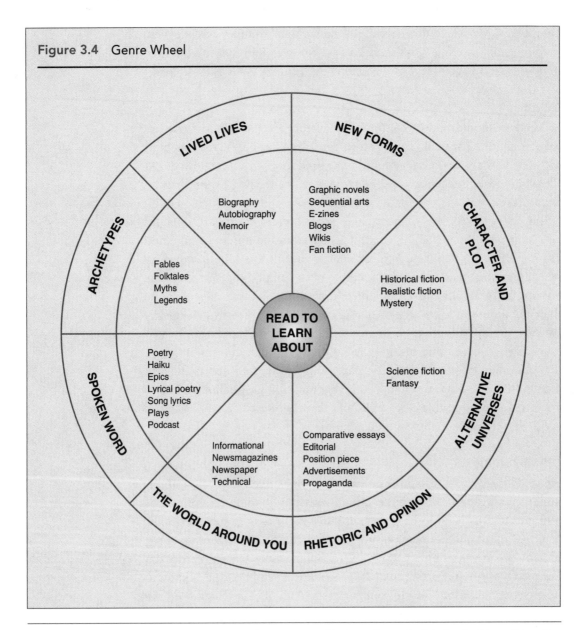

Shifting perspectives can also challenge a reader. The picture book *Yo! Yes?* (Raschka, 1993) bounces the reader back and forth between two boys who carry on a conversation using nearly telegraphic speech. In thirty-four words, they express the hesitancy, fear of rejection, and tentative offers that can be bound up in the uncertainties of making a new friend and then, finally, the celebration of the new bond that is forged between the characters ("Yo! Yes? Hey? Who? You! Me?"). This deceptively simple book requires quite a bit of background knowledge because the reader must shift between these two characters and attend to the spare dialogue, punctuation, font size, and illustrations to make sense of the story.

Narration

Another consideration related to the structure of the text relates to narration. If the point of view shifts in a narrative text, it's likely harder for students to grasp the meaning of that text. For example, in *Rose Blanche* (Innocenti, 1985), the author starts with a first-person narrative, using statements such as "My name is Rose Blanche. I live in a small town in Germany with narrow streets, old fountains and tall houses with pigeons on the roofs" (p. 1). Later in the book, however, the author shifts to third-person narration, and the reader is left to infer what happened to the main character.

Similarly, some authors deliberately construct narrators for the purpose of keeping information hidden from their readers. These can be first- or third-person narrators, and those with limited or omniscient views. For many readers, omniscient narrators make the text easier to understand because the narrator knows everything and reveals things as they become important. When the narrator changes, however, or when the narrator is *unreliable*—as is the case in *The Adventures of Huckleberry Finn* (Twain, 1884) and *One Flew Over the Cuckoo's Nest* (Kesey, 1962)—the reader can be challenged.

Older readers may experience similar shifting perspectives in compilation biographies as well. *We Rode the Orphan Trains* (Warren, 2004) moves frequently between third-person explanations of factual information and first-person recollections. For instance, after two pages of a third-person account about an adoptive four-year-old girl's experience of being chosen by a man who stated, "I need someone to wash the dishes" (p. 4), there is a shift to this recollection from the girl herself, many years later:

> When a couple standing nearby saw what was
> happening, the husband dashed to an ice-cream shop
> and returned with a strawberry cone.
>   He knelt in front of me and asked, "Would you like
> to have this?" His voice was very gentle. "You can have

one every day," he told me. An orphan never turns down food and I took the cone. I can still remember how good it tasted. I put my hand in his hand. He turned to his wife and said, "Minnie, let's take this little girl home." (p. 4)

The change in perspective is sudden, and the only clues a reader has are the extra spaces separating the first-person account from the third-person exposition, with its accompanying change in pronouns. There's no change in font, nor is this different section of text titled or set apart from the surrounding text as a boxed feature. These shifts in perspective can make otherwise straightforward texts complex because the reader must attend to a change in the narration.

Graphic and Visual Information

Finally, the structure of the text can be analyzed in terms of how graphics and visual information, such as text features, are used. In some cases, the graphics used within the text demand attention and are required for understanding. In fact, the Caldecott award from the American Library Association honors the illustrators of picture books whose work "provides the child with a visual experience" and further describes the work as possessing "a collective unity of story-line, theme, or concept, developed through the series of pictures of which the book is comprised" (American Library Association, 2008). This is an important delineation, in recognition of the complexity that visuals can possess. While in some cases the graphic and visual information is used to create a more visually appealing page, truly complex graphics and illustrations are those that are essential to a reader's understanding of the story itself. Take the groundbreaking work of 2008 Caldecott award winner Brian Selznick for his work *The Invention of Hugo Cabret*, which has been described as "a silent film on paper" (Schwartz, 2007). This is an apt description of the 284 illustrations, which must be attended to as carefully as scenes in a film. When the graphics are necessary for understanding, as they are in this novel, the text is more complex than it otherwise might be.

▶ Language Conventionality and Clarity

In addition to considering the levels of meaning and the specific words and phrases that are used in a given text, one must take into account the conventionality and clarity of the language when determining a text's complexity. Some texts are more complex, and thus more difficult for readers, precisely because of complexities that are wrapped up in the nature of the language itself. In some cases, this may be due to the figurative language that is used. But language conventionality and clarity have to do with more than figurative language. As noted on the qualitative measures scale, two additional factors impact text complexity in this area: language variations and registers.

Standard English and Variations

When a reader reads a text that is consistent with his or her language usage, the text is easier; when a reader reads a text that contains variations from the language that he or she uses, the text is harder. Many of the books students are expected to read are written in standard English. If students have sufficient experience with this language form, then the texts are likely easier to understand. If they do not have a lot of experience with standard English, the texts will be more difficult. For example, *Gregor Mendel* (Bardoe, 2006) was written in standard English and includes sentences such as these:

> Enterprising Gregor, by working as a tutor, paid his own way through four more years of school. Even when he was sick, Gregor never fell behind in his lessons. (p. 5)

When a reader reads a text that is consistent with his or her language usage, the text is easier; when a reader reads a text that contains variations from the language that he or she uses, the text is harder.

Speakers of standard English will not likely find this difficult to understand, even though it is formally constructed. English learners and students for whom standard English is less familiar might find this text more challenging, and thus need more instruction to make sense of it.

Other books are written in different vernaculars or variations. These books are authentic, in that they respect the time in which they are set or the language that is in use by the people profiled in the book. For example, reading a conversation between Jim and Huck Finn requires an understanding of the language used at the time and place where the book is set. Consider Malik, a regular user of African American Vernacular English. When he read *The Watsons Go to Birmingham—1963* (Curtis, 1995), the text was not that complex for him. It fit his experiences with language conventions. For example, this passage posed no problem for him:

> "I thought you was my friend. I didn't think you was like all them other people," he said. "I though you was different." He didn't say this stuff like he was mad, he just sounded real, real sad. (p. 44)

But this text was very difficult for Amira, a student from Kenya who does not use African American Vernacular English. She is an English learner who has learned standard English, and the use of *was* instead of *were* threw her off. But the book was not so hard for Devin, a student who moved from rural Alabama to the city. The language conventionality was consistent with his experience growing up in the U.S. South.

Poets regularly violate language conventions for striking effect. Earlier we noted how e. e. cummings bent print and grammar conventions to slow readers down, thus encouraging them to dwell a bit longer on the message he intended. Writers Dr. Seuss and Lewis Carroll are well known for introducing neologisms (nonsense words that may become accepted terms), such as *nerd* and *crunk* for Seuss and *galumphing* and *gimble* for Carroll. Portmanteau words (a term itself coined by Carroll) are those that combine the sounds of two words to form an entirely new one. Reading *simulcast* (*simultaneous* + *broadcast*) or *chortle* (*chuckle* + *snort*) requires a student to draw on knowledge of two terms and consider how the concepts of each intertwine to formulate a new idea.

Registers

In addition, a number of factors are related to the formality of the language used in a text. Sociolinguists describe this phenomenon as language registers, and note that language registers are one of the ways in which social relationships reveal themselves in language: "The concept of register is typically concerned with variations in language conditioned by uses rather than users and involves consideration of the situation or context of use, the purpose, subject-matter, and content of the message, and the relationship between the participants" (Romaine, 1994, p. 20). The more registers a speaker possesses, the more able he or she is to communicate effectively in a variety of settings. There are five generally agreed-upon language registers, including these (e.g., Joos, 1967):

- **Fixed or Frozen.** Fixed speech is reserved for traditions in which the language does not change. Examples of fixed speech include the Pledge of Allegiance, Shakespeare plays, and civil ceremonies such as weddings.
- **Formal.** At the formal level, speech is expected to be presented in complete sentences with specific word usage. Formal language is the standard for work, school,

and business and is more often seen in writing than in speaking. However, public speeches and presentations are expected to be delivered in a formal language register.

- **Consultative.** The third level of language, consultative, is a formal register used in conversations. Less appropriate for writing, consultative language is often used by students in their interactions in the classroom.
- **Casual.** This is the language that is used in conversation with friends. In casual speech, word choice is general, and conversation is dependent upon nonverbal assists, significant background knowledge, and shared information.
- **Intimate.** This is the language used by very close friends and lovers. Intimate speech is private and often requires a significant amount of shared history, knowledge, and experience.

Literary texts using a narrative form trade in all of these registers as a way of demonstrating the relationship characters have with one another. Consider your reading of the dialogue between the squabbling couple in Hemingway's "Hills Like White Elephants." You recognized the intimate register the characters were engaged in and drew conclusions about their attitudes. The unstated tension between the two was a result of your understanding of the register, rather than of a literal reading of the conversation.

Both of these factors, language variation and registers, influence the difficulty a reader may have with a text. Like other qualitative dimensions, they are variables that deserve instructional attention and that teachers need to consider when they are working to ensure that students learn to read texts of sufficient complexity.

▶ Knowledge Demands

Knowledge demand, like other quantitative and qualitative elements of text complexity, laps at the edges of the individual reader himself. All writers presume that their readers possess a certain level of knowledge. These assumptions about knowledge demand can be uncovered through an analysis of the text. More specifically, teachers can come to an understanding of a given text's knowledge demand by examining the level of prior knowledge needed to understand a text, as well as by considering what background knowledge and cultural knowledge may be required of the reader. The degree to which a given text requires formal vocabulary knowledge also plays an important role in determining the level of knowledge demand associated with the text.

Background Knowledge

The life experiences of a reader play a role in his or her understanding of a piece of text. This type of knowledge, called background knowledge, is typically gained informally, and varies from one student to another. When making sense of a text, a reader invariably draws on his or her life experiences about how information is conveyed between people, and about how it is recounted.

When qualitatively analyzing a literary text in relation to students' background knowledge, an examination of the text's content is in order. A simple story about nurturing a living plant or animal as it grows is likely to be an experience familiar to many young children. Conversely, the ability to recognize similar nurturing qualities in Mother Wolf, as she raises Mowgli, a young boy in Rudyard Kipling's *The Jungle Book* (1894/1985), is likely to place more demand on the reader. In this instance, readers would likely be required to move beyond their own direct experiences in order to project these qualities onto the talking wolf. The novel's setting in colonial India also places some distance—in both time and experience—between the text and young readers. As well, the book can be understood through its multiple themes. Younger readers are likely to discern its themes of loyalty and friendship, while older students may look beyond this to recognize the political commentary of British colonialism and the text's position as a moralistic piece when it was first published in 1894.

Prior Knowledge

In addition to the life experiences that students gain, they acquire more formal prior knowledge that must be utilized in order to understand new information in the text. In literary texts, this may be evidenced in a student's understanding of poetic form as she reads *Love That Dog* (Creech, 2001). This sparse novel draws on several famous poems, notably "The Red Wheelbarrow" by William Carlos Williams and "Love That Boy" by Walter Dean Myers. The protagonist mimics both the forms and the poetic language of these and other poems through the use of journal entries. As well, a story slowly unfolds as the boy reveals his own loss, while ostensibly writing to his teacher about the assignments he is required to complete. This novel is deceptively simple, especially because the number of words per page never tops one hundred and can be as few as eight. But this genre-bending book, with its allusions to other texts, makes it more complex than any quantitative readability formula might measure.

Cultural Knowledge

Many texts allude to culturally bound references, and these can be the hardest to detect when one is a member of the culture in question; it is challenging to distance oneself enough from these familiar references to be able to notice them (Ladson-Billings, 2006). For instance, western literature primarily emanates from Judeo-Christian societies, and biblical references abound. Mention a prodigal son or a Good Samaritan, and some students will understand that this refers to a remorseful person or a selfless one. However, others will not. Some students come from other religious backgrounds, or none at all. Others have little experience with how to interpret such references. Still other cultural knowledge demands go beyond belief systems and can include the values, communication styles, and language proficiencies of a community (Ladson-Billings, 2006; Moll, 1992).

Differences between students' experiences and those of the author of the text can contribute to a text's complexity. Further, it is important to note that these cultural knowledge demands don't flow only in one direction. A student reading *Siddhartha* (Hesse, 1922/2011) will be challenged by the novel's cultural knowledge demand about Buddhism, and that will make this text comparatively more difficult for this student than one situated in contemporary times, such as *Breaking Night: A Memoir of Forgiveness, Survival, and My Journey From Homelessness to Harvard* (Murray, 2010). While both texts capture spiritual journeys of a sort, with wisdom won through suffering and sacrifice, the second book is likely to have less of a cultural knowledge demand than the first because of its contemporary timeline and familiar setting. Those cultural knowledge differences that are situated with the learner are discussed in more detail in the next chapter.

Vocabulary Knowledge

Not to be overlooked is the vocabulary demand a text requires. The words and phrases in a text serve as labels for ideas and concepts related to the knowledge demands of that text. Analysis of vocabulary demand requires asking four questions:

- Are there words or phrases that have multiple meanings?
- Do other elements of the text (especially text features) assist the reader?
- Are there domain-specific labels that represent complex concepts?
- Are there context clues that assist the reader in understanding these terms or phrases?

The domain-specific vocabulary used in the book *Guinea Pig Scientists* (Dendy & Boring, 2005) can be challenging: "In addition to the extermination of *Aedes aegypti* as a way to eliminate yellow fever, by 1937 there was a vaccination against the disease. Dr. Max Theiler helped develop the vaccine with the Rockefeller Foundation. It was called '17D' and is still used to protect people from yellow fever" (p. 83). There is a heavy knowledge demand in these three sentences, with vocabulary serving as labels for complex ideas such as *extermination* (of an insect), *elimination* (of a disease), vaccination (to prevent contracting the disease), and even the source of funding (*the Rockefeller Foundation*). However, at least one text feature, the italicized Latin word, helps the reader understand that the authors are discussing the target of the disease. The reader may or may not have enough language or content knowledge regarding this or other diseases to know that *Aedes aegypti* is an insect. However, the context clues (*protect people* contextualizes *vaccination*, *disease* contextualizes *yellow fever*) provide additional support for the reader.

▶ Returning to *The Hunger Games*, Qualitatively

In Chapter 2, we used a passage from *The Hunger Games* to highlight the various ways that readability formulas work. Recall that the readability of the book overall is 5.3 grade level, with content recommended for Grades 7 and above. To consider the book qualitatively, we need to evaluate it using the factors previously identified, through the use of the scale for qualitatively evaluating literary texts (Figure 3.2).

Levels of Meaning and Purpose

The text focuses on a society in the near-distant future, probably in North America, which has experienced some event that has altered life as it was formerly known. There is a literal story about children who are selected to fight one another to the death, with the winner bringing glory to his or her district. There is a much deeper level of the text that relates to war, government control, reality entertainment, poverty, and family bonds. The figurative language demands of the text are not extensive, but there are flashbacks and foreshadowing that readers must attend to if they are to fully grasp the text. There are some concepts, especially those regarding the traditions and customs of this new world, that may confuse students.

Structure

The genre is likely familiar for students, as dystopian novels are popular with adolescents and young adults (e.g., *The Giver*, the *Divergent* series, and *Feed*, to name a few). The text is told from a first-person narrator perspective. Naturally, the first-person narrator is not omniscient, and thus events unfold for the reader as they do for the narrator. As we noted when discussing the levels of meaning of *The Hunger Games*, there are a number of flashbacks that can confuse adolescent readers, but these are handled well and fairly clearly identified as such. The organization of the text follows the story grammar structure that readers expect, and there are clear conflicts that are resolved.

Language Conventionality and Clarity

There are unfamiliar concepts in *The Hunger Games*, such as a mockingjay (a portmanteau), but they are vividly described and explained. Overall, the language is conventional, with extensive dialogue used to forward the plot. Imagery and descriptions are used to describe the setting and events such that clarity is provided, yet the reader has to visualize a different world in the future. The narrator is conversational and appealing to young adults, in terms of both her actions and her thoughts.

Knowledge Demands

The text places a fairly significant demand on the reader's knowledge base. Although readers will likely have prior knowledge of the genre, and some background knowledge about families and society, the text charts new ground in terms presenting a future world and explaining how decisions are made and how different districts interact with one another within the nation. The major themes—issues with moral dilemmas, government control over citizens, allegiances, war, and hunger—require readers' attention and reflection. There are many unique features of the world in which the main character Katniss lives. This is part of the appeal of the book and one of the reasons that it is more challenging, as readers must actively construct this imaginary world.

In reflecting on these qualitative aspects of the text, it seems reasonable to suggest that it is appropriate for middle school students. That said, there are many middle school students who do not have the background knowledge necessary to fully appreciate the themes that are developed within the text, which is probably why the book is also appealing to high school students and adults. In this case, the qualitative and quantitative analyses are suggesting a similar audience.

▶ Cautions About Qualitative Analysis of Text

Most discussions of quantitative measures of text complexity include a call for qualitative reviews of the text itself. As Hiebert (2011) noted, "Once quantitative data establish that particular texts are 'within the ballpark,' the hard work of qualitatively analyzing the demands of texts in relation to different readers and tasks begins" (pp. 2–3). That being so, there are some concerns about qualitative analyses as well—the first of which has to do with the amount of time that teachers have available to complete these types of reviews. Prominent reading researchers are calling for the development of a national database of greatly expanded exemplars, text maps, and annotated qualitative evaluations so that teachers can access information about teaching points (Pearson & Hiebert, 2014). It is much faster to rely solely on readability formulas, but that type of analysis is limited in that it does not provide the teacher with information about why and how a text may be challenging, and therefore what tasks should be designed to bridge the gaps in student understanding. Understanding the intricacies of all of the various difficulties inherent in a given text is important because teachers can then use that information in lesson planning. We are not suggesting that teachers simply analyze texts and then avoid using hard ones with their students. Instead, we are suggesting that teachers analyze texts to develop text–task relationships, and that they then plan instruction accordingly so that students are stretched to develop the skills that will enable them to read increasingly complex texts on their own (Mesmer, 2007).

Another caution regarding the qualitative analysis of text complexity has to do with the fact that validated tools are few and far between. Chall, Bissex, Conard, and Harris-Sharples (1996) used scaled text exemplars,

What people think of as "normal" varies, based on experience and expertise. A teacher who has worked with affluent, high-performing students may rate a text differently than a teacher who has supported struggling readers.

criteria, and benchmarks to allow teachers to assess a piece of text qualitatively; however, they were not able to complete validation studies on their tools. In the absence of validated tools, teachers should use indicators such as the scale provided in Figure 3.2. Eventually, validated tools will be developed, and there will be new ways to think about qualitative text complexity—but students cannot wait for those tools to be created.

Finally, because students and classrooms vary, the qualitative measures may reflect the expectations of teachers. What people think of as "normal" varies, based on experience and expertise. A teacher who has worked with affluent, high-performing students for thirty years may rate a text differently than a teacher who has effectively supported struggling readers over his or her career. Understanding how texts are complex will help us all teach and reach students based on high expectations, rather than leaving us to exist with the tyranny of low expectations.

▶ Conclusion

Qualitative measures of text complexity can be used in conjunction with quantitative measures to determine the appropriateness of a text for a particular reader and task. There has been a long history of analyzing texts qualitatively, in an effort to determine how students can learn to read increasingly complex and worthy texts. When teachers analyze texts for levels of meaning or purpose, structure, language conventionality and clarity, and knowledge demands, they can use the knowledge they glean to plan appropriate instruction and strategically guide the development of their learners.

Qualitative Aspects of Informational Texts

Learning about the physical, social, and biological world is an important aspect of the curriculum in most of today's schools. Students are expected to read, write, and think about history and other social sciences, physical and life sciences, and a wide range of technical subjects. From the time they enter school until they transition to college and then on to careers, students are immersed in the world of information. That's to say not that literary texts should be neglected, but rather that informational texts are an essential aspect of the curriculum. Unfortunately, in the push to increase students' reading proficiency, some schools and districts have cut down—or even entirely removed—blocks of time for social studies and science (e.g., Howard, 2003).

We see this as wrongheaded because informational texts, such as those used in history and science, facilitate students' reading development, help shape students' understanding of the world, and build their habits of inquiry (Maloch & Horsey, 2013). Fortunately, helping students learn from informational texts, not just textbooks, has received a great deal of attention in the last decade. Facilitating students' exposure to and engagement with these texts can help them focus on building content-area vocabulary knowledge and study skills and on becoming proficient with the use of tools such as graphic organizers and note-taking guides (Altieri, 2011). These valuable knowledge and skill sets are important avenues through which students can refine their habits for interacting with—and understanding—informational texts.

▶ Characteristics of Informational Texts

Facilitating students' exposure to and engagement with informational texts can help them focus on building content-area vocabulary knowledge and study skills.

Informational texts rely primarily on exposition rather than narration. As noted in the previous chapter, we do not sort informational and literary text types into fiction and nonfiction, because it obscures the differences in text construction. Literary texts, whether true or imagined, typically employ narrative forms. Informational texts describe, explain, and inform the reader. Biographies and auto-biographies, for instance, use a narrative form to convey experiences, and because of that, their structure is best analyzed using the literary text scale in the previous chapter (see Figure 3.2). Informational texts, particularly documents, encyclopedia entries, reference books, technical guides, scientific journal articles, reports, and question-and-answer text, use exposition. Unlike narrative forms, which are primarily linear (i.e., there is a beginning, a middle, and an end to the story), informational texts are nonlinear. Instead, their major point of organization centers on a process or phenomenon.

Informational texts that use an expository form are characterized by elements that can challenge a reader's comprehension. All texts, oral as well as written, can be analyzed by considering the field, tenor, and mode of a piece (Halliday, 1985). *Field* refers to the topic or subject of the text, and answers the question, "What is the text about?" Informational text fields cover the physical, biological, and social worlds, and are commonly used in science, history/social science, mathematics, and technical subjects.

The *tenor* of a text describes the relationship between the writer and the reader. The tenor of informational texts is typically authoritative and may be somewhat socially distant. Writers of informational texts written for younger readers, or for novices on a given topic, may bridge this social distance by making the text more personal, addressing the reader directly (i.e., use of personal pronouns such as *I* and *you*). Writers of informational texts may convey their expertise through the accuracy of the text and may also adopt a stance that does or does not allow the reader to disagree with the text. The *mode* of a text answers the question, "How was this produced?" A speech, for instance, functions foremost in its oral form, although it has a secondary written form as well. The writer of a newspaper article might have interviewed others about a topic, but reported the outcomes of these discussions more formally than when they were initially conducted face-to-face. A scientific journal article functions solely in written form, and is therefore a much more formal mode. Each of these modes carries with it an expectation of how the information will be organized. Mode also describes the rhetorical nature of the text: is it meant to inform, to persuade, or to make an argument through the use of formal reasoning? Taken together, the variables of field, tenor, and mode describe the register of academic writing, with each contributing to the complexity of an informational text.

▶ Analyzing Informational Texts Qualitatively

Given the unique characteristics of informational texts that use exposition, we have developed a second complexity scale for this text type. The impetus to do so was Sherrye Dee Garrett at Texas A&M University–Corpus Christi and two of her students, Jeannette Gomez and Lindsay Bingaman. While they found the qualitative scale published in the first edition of this book to be useful for analyzing literary texts, they struggled with using it for informational texts that relied on exposition. This led to a rich discussion among them about the nature of informational texts, and they ultimately produced the scale found in Figure 4.1. The intent of this scale is to reflect Halliday's (1985) model of analyzing texts through the lens of field, tenor, and mode. In order to increase its ease of use, the scale is organized into the same categories, with one exception, which is the substitution of the category of narration for that of voice.

Figure 4.1 Qualitative Scale of Informational Texts

Score	1 point (Comfortable) Texts That Are Comfortable and/or Build Background, Fluency, and Skills	2 points (Grade Level) Texts That Require Grade-Appropriate Skills	3 points (Stretch) Texts That Would Stretch a Reader and/or Require Instruction
Levels of Meaning and Purpose			
Density and Complexity	Single and literal levels of meaning are present; meaning is explicitly stated.	Multiple layers of specific content are present. Some information must be inferred or integrated with previous content.	Significant density and complexity, with multiple layers of content topics, are present. The reader is expected to critique or evaluate information.
Analogies and Abstract Comparisons	There is limited use of analogous statements. Language relies on literal interpretations.	Analogies and metaphors are used to help the reader make connections between new concepts and the reader's knowledge. These associations draw on familiar processes and phenomena.	The metaphors and analogies used are more abstract and require sophistication and depth of knowledge from the reader. The process or phenomenon used to make a comparison itself requires prior knowledge.
Purpose	The purpose is directly and explicitly stated at the beginning of the text and is in evidence throughout the text.	The text serves both explicit and implicit purposes, which become evident with close inspection of the text.	The text may involve multiple purposes, some of which may be implicit; it requires the reader to critically analyze across texts to discern implicit purposes.
Structure			
Genre	The text exemplifies conventional characteristics of one familiar genre.	The text exemplifies one genre, but deviates from typical characteristics of that genre.	The text is presented as a specific genre, but includes other embedded genres.
Organization	One conventional organizational pattern predominates throughout the text. Signal words and phrases are overt and numerous.	More than one conventional organization pattern is included in the text. Signal words and phrases are present.	The text may include a variety of conventional organizational patterns, which are dictated by text content, but with little notification or guidance to the reader.

Score	1 point (Comfortable) Texts That Are Comfortable and/or Build Background, Fluency, and Skills	2 points (Grade Level) Texts That Require Grade-Appropriate Skills	3 points (Stretch) Texts That Would Stretch a Reader and/or Require Instruction
Text Features	The text contains familiar access features such as a table of contents, headings/subheadings, a glossary, and an index.	The text contains conventional access features, but also includes detailed information in sidebars, insets, and bulleted lists.	The text contains access features that require the reader to integrate extratextual information, such as preface/prologue, afterword/epilogue, and author/illustrator notes.
Graphic Elements	The text contains familiar graphic elements such as simple diagrams, maps, timelines, photographs, and illustrations with captions. Graphic elements repeat information in the text.	The text contains graphic elements that require interpretation, such as graphs and tables, scale diagrams, and webs. Graphic elements have additional information that supplements the text.	The text contains graphic elements that are less familiar to students and require interpretation, such as cross sections, cutaways, and range and flow maps. Graphic elements have information that complements and is integrated with text.
Language Conventionality and Clarity			
Language Level	The language used is appropriate to the developmental and experiential level of the student.	There is some distance between the text language and the developmental and experiential language level of the student.	The text language uses language conventions and structures unfamiliar to the student, especially those that reflect voices found in specific content areas.
Register	The register is casual and familiar. Humorous language may be used throughout to engage the reader in the information.	The register is consultative or formal, and may be academic, but acknowledges the developmental level of the reader. Humorous or casual language may be used in titles and headings/subheadings.	The register is domain-specific, formal, and/or scholarly.

(Continued)

Figure 4.1 (Continued)

Score	1 point (Comfortable) Texts That Are Comfortable and/or Build Background, Fluency, and Skills	2 points (Grade Level) Texts That Require Grade-Appropriate Skills	3 points (Stretch) Texts That Would Stretch a Reader and/or Require Instruction
Voice	Information in the text is presented in a straightforward way. Text may use second-person language and a personal tone to draw the reader into the text.	Vocabulary and diction invite the reader's curiosity about the text content while presenting information with an authoritative tone.	Strong authoritative voice dominates the text. Text language is used to impart knowledge to the reader and makes little effort to engage the reader on a personal level.
Knowledge Demands			
Background Knowledge	The content closely matches the reader's primary lived experiences and secondary experiences gained through other media.	The content represents a distance between the reader's primary and secondary experiences, but the text provides explanations to bridge the gap between what is known and unknown.	The content demands specialized knowledge beyond the primary and secondary experiences of the reader and provides no bridge or scaffolding between known and unknown.
Prior Knowledge	Prior knowledge is needed to understand the text, which is familiar and draws on a solid foundation of practical, general, and academic learning.	Subject-specific knowledge is required but is augmented with review or summary of information.	Specialized or technical content knowledge is presumed; little review or explanation of these concepts is present in the text.
Vocabulary Knowledge	The vocabulary is controlled and uses the most commonly held meanings; multiple-meaning words are used in a limited fashion.	The vocabulary draws on domain-specific, general academic, and multiple-meaning words, with text supports to guide the reader's correct interpretations of their meanings; it represents familiar concepts and ideas.	The vocabulary demand is extensive, domain-specific, and representative of complex ideas; little is offered in the way of context clues.

Source: Adapted by Sherrye Dee Garrett, Jeannette Gomez, and Lindsay Bingaman.

▶ Levels of Meaning and Purpose

Like narrative texts, informational texts can have surface levels of meaning as well as deeper implications. Informational texts often present facts and dates, but the reading of this information is not always straightforward. Often, the author provides factual information for the reader to consider and includes ideas and perspectives that challenge the reader.

Density and Complexity

Density refers primarily to lexical density and conceptual load. Lexical density is increased when words are nominalized, meaning that a verb or adjective is turned into a noun. Science and social science texts are loaded with nominalizations (*resist* becomes *resistance, different* becomes *difference*). When affixes are applied, the terms become even more challenging (*careless* becomes *carelessness*). In addition, informational texts feature technical terms associated with the topic. For example, a passage about the periodic table of elements is likely to contain words and phrases such as *isotopes, instability, atomic number,* and *electron configurations*. Now factor in the conceptual load—that is, the number of ideas—that are packed into a few sentences.

By way of example, this short passage appears in *The Story of Money* (Maestro, 1995), which has a quantitative measure of 890L, a score measuring the factors that can be quantified, thus placing it in the Grade 4–5 range:

> The world has entered an electronic age and the latest form of cashless money is stored in bank computers. People can have their paychecks electronically added to their bank accounts. Their bills can then be paid directly by the bank using advanced communication systems. No actual money changes hands.

A number of content-specific terms are used (*cashless money, paychecks, bank accounts*), as well as a nominalization (*communication*). In addition, the conceptual load includes abstract ideas ("The world has entered an electronic age," and paychecks are "electronically added" to bank accounts, through "advanced communication systems"). And just to make it a little bit more dense, let's add some figurative language: "no actual money changes hands." Those four sentences cram a lot of information into a very short passage, with little elaboration or restatement.

Many informational texts—especially those that focus on a single topic—have a clear, explicit meaning. More complex texts may include nuanced information about the topic and related issues, and may reveal the writer's attitude toward the subject, thereby inviting the reader to evaluate and critique the information. The book *Shark Attack!* (Tuchman, 2013) is written for second-grade reading instruction. The first part of the book provides factual information about sharks' history, sizes, habitat, and food sources. The later pages say that sharks are both "terrifying and beautiful" (p. 28) and we should "keep the seas swimming with supercool sharks" (p. 29). This language goes beyond facts and presents the author's attitude about shark conservation and protection. Readers need to be ready to evaluate the different levels of meaning that may be present in a text.

Analogies and Abstract Comparisons

In general, informational texts do not employ the wide range of figurative language found in literary ones—at least in the conventional sense. However, writers of informational texts commonly use similes, metaphors, and analogies to compare a familiar process or phenomenon to an unfamiliar, abstract concept. This assists readers in linking their prior knowledge to new information.

In *Blood*, an informational text for elementary students, the author writes that "[r]ed blood cells are like delivery trucks that begin at the heart, then make their first stop at the lungs" (Ring, 2002, p. 12). In a *Scientific American* article titled "Untangling the Roots of Cancer," the writer states that "[t]he immediate cause of cancer must be some combination of insults and accidents that induces normal cells in a healthy human body to turn malignant, growing like weeds and sprouting in unnatural places" (Gibbs, 2003). These analogies work well when they are understood by the reader, but they also tax the reader to rapidly analyze the properties or processes the writer is referring to, and then apply them abstractly to newer information. In other words, the reader needs to be able to determine the degree to which the characteristics of one property or process are similar to those of another. For this reason, analogies and other metaphors used to represent abstract processes may need to be highlighted.

Purpose

The complexity of an informational text is increased when the purpose is not clearly stated, or when the apparent purpose differs from the stated purpose. There is a wide range of informational texts that do not have an explicitly stated purpose, such as *Animal Disguises* (Weber, 2004). It's clear that this book about camouflage in nature provides information for the reader, but it does not come right out and tell you what the purpose is and what to expect. Accordingly, it is a little more complex than a book that explicitly says something like, "In this section, we will focus on camouflage as one of the ways that animals can disguise themselves."

Comparisons between multiple texts can also reveal conflicting purposes, and speeches and other historical documents often chronicle these implicit and explicit purposes, especially in light of events that serve to contextualize their creation. Those delivered by leaders during times of war are often ripe for discussion about stated and implicit purposes. For example, General Dwight D. Eisenhower wrote a message to the Allied troops dated June 6, 1944, as they embarked on the D-Day invasion. It was inspiring, and the general conveyed his confidence in their skills. But tellingly, he also drafted a memo to be delivered in the event the operation failed, suggesting that even as he composed the former, he was also preparing for the worst. By comparing these two documents with the historical record, students are able to see how Eisenhower's purposes for both are revealed (Fisher & Frey, 2013).

▶ Structure

All texts are governed by organizational structures that allow readers to experience the ideas or information coherently. Narrative forms rely on a story grammar structure, while informational texts use exposition. These organizing principles are further realized and expressed through specific genres characteristic of the field, all of which employ expository text types to create a comprehensible flow of information. The structure and organization of a given text is also further enhanced through the use of text features and graphic elements.

Genre

In part, texts within a specific genre may present as difficult to students, depending on their past reading experiences with these genres. If students have a lot of experiences with reading and using a procedural text to assemble an item, for example, then another text in that genre may be easier for them to manage. Alternatively, if they have not had a lot of experience with persuasive speeches, for instance, then understanding Martin Luther King's "I Have a Dream" speech will be more difficult. Recognizing this is particularly important in the elementary grades, where young students historically have had limited experience with informational texts (Duke, 2000). Informational text genres are frequently more difficult than literary ones, in part because students have been undertaught the conventions or style of a particular text.

Texts within a specific genre may present as difficult to students, depending on their past reading experiences with these genres.

At a more discrete level, students should recognize textual sub-genres and traits that are associated with a discipline (Shanahan & Shanahan, 2008). For example, historical texts include primary and secondary sources. Primary sources were not written for schoolchildren, and are often more challenging because students are not the intended audience. Some primary source documents are edited to facilitate comprehension, while others are left in their original form. Consider the preamble to the U.S. Constitution, arguably one of our nation's most important documents:

> We the People of the United States, in Order to form a more perfect Union, establish Justice, insure domestic Tranquility, provide for the common defense, promote the general Welfare, and secure the Blessings of Liberty to ourselves and our Posterity, do ordain and establish this Constitution for the United States of America.

While not an easy read, it is worthy of a reader's efforts to understand it in its original form. Students may, for instance, struggle with ideas in the preamble that relate to the text's genre (historical document) as well as to the time of its development: the questions of who the *"we"* is referring to, why some words are capitalized, what domestic tranquility is, why "more perfect" was selected rather than "perfect."

In science, different or alternative representations of an idea (e.g., pictures, graphs or charts, text, or diagrams) are essential for a full understanding of the concepts. Readers of science genre texts (reports, lab results, visual representations of quantitative data) must continually move back and forth between text and visuals to fully understand the concepts presented. Scientific information is also found in reference books, which may require the reader to search an online encyclopedia for technical information about a term. Unlike lab results, which should invite a critique, the definition of *mollusk* should not. Science students need instruction on when and how to critique certain genres, while recognizing when more objective information sources are used.

Organization

In terms of structure, there is significant evidence that the manner in which a text's ideas or topics are arranged and related impacts students' comprehension (Bakken & Whedon, 2002; Ciardiello, 2002; Parsons, 2001). The most common informational text structures are as follows:

- **Descriptive.** Rich and detailed information about a process, procedure, action, or phenomenon is presented.
- **Compare and Contrast.** Similarities and differences between two concepts are explained.
- **Temporal Sequence.** Events change or remain the same over time, and are explained in chronological order.
- **Cause and Effect.** An event is explained in terms of its effect, using temporal precedence (i.e., a cause must occur before the effect).
- **Problem and Solution.** A problematic situation or issue is presented, as is an explanation of how it was resolved.

The different structures are often signaled to readers through the use of key words and phrases. Words that signal a descriptive/list organization include *for example* and *in addition*, and may even include enumerated facts. Signal words and phrases for a text with a compare/contrast organization include *however* and *on the other hand*. Cause-and-effect structures are signaled to the reader through use of terms such as *because, consequently*, and *for this reason*. Texts with a problem-and-solution organization prompt careful readers by using signal words and phrases like *one answer is, this led to, the dilemma is*, and *to solve this*. Signal words and phrases clearly convey the structure of a given text and help readers process information.

However, the prominence of signal words and phrases in elementary texts gives way to more subtle methods of presenting the information, and it becomes less common to see them being used as frequently in middle and high school texts. While middle and high school texts of course continue to follow the rules of organization, their structure may not be as overt, stretching the reader to infer the organizational pattern.

Some texts have a dominant and obvious structure, such as *A Wasp Is Not a Bee* (Singer, 1995), which uses a compare-and-contrast organization to explain similarities and differences between animal pairs. Other texts may have multiple patterns, but signal words help the reader navigate the complexity. One factor that ensures that texts are comprehensible is the development and explanation of concepts, phenomena, and events in a logical and straightforward manner. When achieved, texts with these attributes embody a concept known as *coherence*—that is, they possess a systematic or logical connection or consistency. As with structure, there is significant evidence that the level of coherence of a given text is an important consideration in determining its level of difficulty (McNamara & Kintsch, 1996).

Informational texts are typically organized using one or more of these expository structures. When this is the case, and readers have experiences with these structures, the reading is more comfortable. When authors do not use as many signal words, or where the coherence is diminished due to the scope of the information, readers have to work a little harder. *Inside the* Titanic (Marschall, 1997) provides readers with information in chronological order, with clear timelines and corresponding information. This is easier to read than *Bury the Dead: Tombs, Corpses, Mummies, Skeletons, and Rituals* (Sloan, 2002) because even though it also has timelines, they stretch over thousands of years, cross many continents, and explore a range of concepts and thematic strands (geography, history, culture, biology). In contrast, *Inside the* Titanic focuses on a shorter period in history and one central idea. While both books fall quantitatively into the Grade 6–8 range, one is harder than the other, based on the organization used.

Just as authors have different ways of establishing a text's organization, so too do they have a number of ways of specifically addressing the issue of text coherence. For example, when main ideas are explicitly stated and in an obvious place at the start of each section, readers are more likely to understand the information. Second, when the information found within a paragraph or section is clearly connected back to the main idea, coherence is improved. Third, when there is a logical order of events and there are obvious relationships between events and topics, comprehension is easier and more likely to occur. Fourth, when readers are provided with clear references and referents and ambiguous pronouns are avoided, texts are easier. And finally, when there are seamless transitions between topics, reading is smooth and feels comfortable.

Text Features

Informational texts using an expository form do not tell a story in the linear fashion associated with narrative. Instead, information is presented as it pertains to separate but related topics or subtopics. In order to guide readers through and across topics, writers of expository texts employ a variety of text features. Readers' familiarity with some of these features—basic elements, such as a table of contents, major headings, a glossary, and an index—enables them to navigate the presentation of information in an expository text. More sophisticated texts require more from the reader. Sidebars, insets, and bulleted lists are all examples of features that require readers to attend to information located on different parts of the same page, breaking their engagement with the natural flow of text. In these instances, readers must take information from several locations on the same page and infer the relationship between that and the main text. Still other informational text forms expect the reader to use information outside of the main body of text, such as a prologue, a preface, author's notes, and bibliographies.

There are a number of additional text features that authors and editors may use to serve as organizational markers. For example, headings and subheadings can guide readers through information. Similarly, margin notes, graphic organizers, structured overviews, text maps, and the like can provide readers with an alternative way to understand the information being presented. Different text features, such as bold words and charts, serve different purposes.

Graphic Elements

The information presented in many informational texts is made clearer through the effective use of graphic elements. Moline (2012) observes, "There are times when it makes sense *not* to write information in sentences. Visual texts sometimes do the job better" (p. 10). It would take many words and complicated sentences, for example, to describe the design and use of bones throughout the human body. However, books like *Body Basics: Bones* (Ganeri, 2009) provide diagrams, cutaways, illustrations, photographs, and X-rays of various bone systems in the body. Each section has a main text block, labeled graphic elements, and a facts insert. Twist's (2011) *A Little Book of Slime: Everything That Oozes, From Killer Slime to Living Mold* also includes a "slime-ometer" that requires readers to interpret information in a graphic that is analogous to a weather thermometer. *Micromonsters: Creatures That Live on Your Skin, in Your Hair, and in Your Home!* (Jackson, 2010) uses scaled diagrams so the reader can determine the actual size of the creature discussed. Individual graphic elements are often not difficult to read by themselves; the complexity comes into play when readers must make connections between the different kinds of information that are spread out visually on the page. Readers often need instruction when it comes to interpreting the information presented within graphic/visual elements, such as graphs, diagrams, cutaways, and scale indicators; they also need support in putting these separate pieces of text together. As discussed, both text features and graphic elements contribute to a text's organizational structure. A summary of some common text features and graphic elements and their functions can be found in Figure 4.2.

Figure 4.2 Common Text Features and Graphic Elements and Their Functions

Function	Text Features
Elements that organize	• Chapters • Titles • Headings • Subheadings • List of figures
Elements for locating information	• Table of contents • Indexes • Page numbers
Elements for explanation and elaboration	• Diagrams • Charts and tables • Graphs • Glossary
Elements that illustrate	• Photographs • Illustrations
Elements that notify	• Bolded words • Italics and other changes in font

Source: Fisher, Frey, & Lapp (2008a).

▶ Language Conventionality and Clarity

Informational texts generally do not involve the variations of standard English, vernacular, or dialect that you would find in some literary texts involving different characters and cultures. However, the tenor of the text (i.e., the relationship between reader and author) is strongly influenced by the way language is used, and by how the reader is addressed. A reader's ability to comprehend an informational text is made more difficult when there are gaps between the text's academic language use and the student's own. It is in this way that the voice and register impart the tenor of the text.

Language Level

The level or degree of sophistication of language in informational text varies based on its intended audience. Texts written for elementary students, for instance, use language that is similar to the students' experiential level. Text progressions allow for the increased use of complex sentences, which often make use of embedded phrases or clauses. Compare two passages, the first from Piaget's seminal work on the language and thinking of children, and the second from a book used in high school psychology courses, discussing the work:

> An adult is at once more highly individualized and far more highly socialized than a child forming part of such a society. He is more individualized, since he can work in private without announcing what he is doing, and without imitating his neighbours. . . . The child is neither individualized, since he cannot keep a single thought secret, and since everything done by one member of the group is repeated through a sort of imitative repercussion by almost every other member, nor is he socialized, since this imitation is not accompanied by what may properly be called an interchange of thought, about half the remarks made by children being ego-centric in character. (Piaget, 1974, p. 61)

The passage below is from the book for high school students:

> Part of the reason for the egocentricity of children is that a significant part of their language involves gestures, movements, and sounds. As these are not words, they cannot express everything, so children must remain partly a prisoner of their own mind. We can understand this when we appreciate that the greater an adult's mastery of language, the more likely they are to be able to understand, or at least be aware of, the views of others. Language, in fact, takes people beyond

A reader's ability to comprehend an informational text is made more difficult when there are gaps between the text's academic language use and the student's own.

themselves, which is why human culture puts such stress on teaching it to children—it enables them to eventually move out of egocentric thinking. (Butler-Bowdon, 2007, p. 224)

Piaget, of course, was not writing for a high school audience; he was writing for other scientists. The second author expanded the ideas expressed in Piaget's work (including that sixty-seven-word sentence) and added further explanation and elaboration. He also reduced the number of technical terms and drew on his sense of the reader's existing knowledge to match the language level to the reader. This example, like many others, draws on other qualitative factors, including register, discussed next.

Register

Informational texts reflect registers from the casual to the formal, sometimes within the same book. A casual register is often used for the title and table of contents in order to engage the reader. Huggins-Cooper's (2008) *Awesome Animals: Beastly Birds and Bats* offers intriguing section titles like "Putrid Pellets," "Dirty Defenses," and "Stinky Birds." These catchy titles are often a gateway to more consultative and formal language in the body texts of the books. When readers turn to the "Stinky Birds" section, they find fairly straightforward information: "The hoopoe makes a foul-smelling nest in a hole in a tree trunk or wall. It adds lots of feces to the nest to keep predators away" (p. 23).

Similarly, Branzei's (2002) *Grossology: The Science of Really Gross Things* is followed by a table of contents with three subdivisions: "Slimy, Mushy, Oozy Gross Things," "Crusty, Scaly Gross Things," and "Stinky, Smelly Gross Things." The text itself uses humor and a casual register, combined with more formal language:

Snot is one part of your daily diet that you never think about. Snot? Yep, you swallow about a quart of it each day. . . . Snot is a slippery liquid called nose mucus (MEW cuss) mixed with a special bacteria-killing chemical. (p. 32)

Then there are those texts that use a formal register throughout. The passage from Piaget is one example. Gray's (2009) book *The Elements:*

A Visual Exploration of Every Known Atom in the Universe is another. It contains beautiful photographs and graphic elements and functions primarily as a reference, rather than as a text likely to be consumed from beginning to end. The register is formal and didactic, as most reference works are. An example from the section on vanadium:

> Tool, steel and high-speed steel are families of iron (26) alloys distinguished by their supreme hardness, toughness, and wear resistance, properties contributed by a few percent of vanadium in the form of vanadium carbide. (p. 63)

Voice

An author's voice conveys a tone—an attitude—toward the subject matter or the reader. An author's voice can be serious and foreboding, or it can be light, humorous, or sarcastic. Even factual information can be presented with a specific voice. Leon's (2001) *Uppity Women of the New World* conveys the author's attitude toward societal views of women in the title, and that attitude continues in the text. What separates this informational text from narrative forms like biography is the extensive use of information to bolster the author's argument. In a passage about Mary Katherine Goddard, who became Baltimore's first postmaster in 1775, Leon reports that

> [a]fter fourteen years running the post office, Mary K. lost her job. Cutbacks? Hardly. Now that it was a cushy federal post with a travel expense account, bureaucrats thought the job "too difficult for a woman." (pp. 29–30)

In another section of book, the author writes:

> From today's perspective, however, the greatest barrier broken by women during these tumultuous times was that of racism: their rebel attitudes ranged from the courage of early "underground railroad" activist Anna Douglass to the splendid insouciance of Elizabeth Mumbet Freeman, a slave who in 1783 stood up in court and demanded to be free, as spelled out in her own state's new constitution. (p. 3)

The writer clearly telegraphs her attitude, using terms like *courage* and *insouciance* in her description of the events, and embeds a quote about the job being too difficult to punctuate her disagreement with this decision. In fact, you can almost hear the writer's sarcastic tone in selecting this quote.

Informational texts can also vary in the degree to which they make use of an authoritative voice, and this then becomes another factor that plays into the tenor of the text. Formal academic text is traditionally written in the third person, and the writer rarely addresses the reader. In contrast, Butler-Bowden's (2007) use of the word *we* in his explanation of Piaget's findings is invitational, and the reader is made to feel as though he or she is a junior colleague. Other writers intentionally adopt a second-person stance to directly address the reader, reaching across the so-called fourth wall that divides reader and author.

Franklin Watts publishes a history series with serious-but-not-too-serious titles that begin with *You Wouldn't Want to . . . (Work on the Great Wall of China, Be a Mayan Soothsayer*, etc.). The series takes a familiar tone by addressing the reader in second person. These books have cartoon-like illustrations to convey a tongue-in-cheek tone, which is contrasted with substantive facts and details. One example is *You Wouldn't Want to Be an American Pioneer! A Wilderness You'd Rather Not Tame* (Morley, 2002). The introduction places the reader in the position of being a farmer who is traveling west in the 1840s. All the facts in the books are presented in the familiar second-person voice: "Dig a well to reach underground water. You will pass lots of wells dug by previous pioneers" (p. 18).

For informational texts in particular, there can be an authoritative voice that appears to have credibility based on experiences conveyed or examples provided. In many cases, the use of the second person fulfills a different purpose: to convey expertise. Therefore, the writer may speak directly to the reader, as in "you will notice" or "when you assume too much," which serves to reengage the reader because the perspective left with the reader is that the author is speaking to him or her. This technique is not as common in literary forms, but informational texts can successfully use the second-person point of view to reduce the text difficulty level. If a reader cannot perceive the nuances of attitude and tone presented by the author, however, he or she may not fully comprehend the information. The complexity lies not only in the information itself but also in the reader's ability or inability to interpret the author's voice.

▶ Knowledge Demands

The final factors for qualitatively evaluating informational texts address the extent to which the material corresponds with the knowledge of the intended audience. In other words, audience appropriateness is a measure of how well the text matches the students' probable background and prior knowledge (Fisher & Frey, 2009). These are two important factors for consideration. Some writers consider how much information their reader already knows and can then "elaborate new concepts sufficiently to be meaningful to readers and to facilitate learning" (Armbruster, 1996, p. 54). The research on audience appropriateness is particularly strong (Alexander, Schallert, & Hare, 1991; Seda, Ligouri, & Seda, 1999) and clearly indicates that this should be a major point of consideration when determining the appropriateness of a given text.

Prior Knowledge

Informational texts, particularly discipline-specific ones, can also be made more complex depending on the amount of formal academic knowledge needed to understand the reading. Consider, for instance, the amount of prior knowledge needed to understand Franklin Delano Roosevelt's "Pearl Harbor Address to the Nation" speech on December 8, 1941. After declaring that the previous day would "live in infamy," the president continued:

> The United States was at peace with that nation and, at the solicitation of Japan, was still in conversation with its government and its emperor looking toward the maintenance of peace in the Pacific.
>
> Indeed, one hour after Japanese air squadrons had commenced bombing in the American island of Oahu, the Japanese ambassador to the United States and his colleague delivered to our Secretary of State a formal reply to a recent American message. And while this reply stated that it seemed useless to continue the existing diplomatic negotiations, it contained no threat or hint of war or of armed attack. (History Matters, n.d.)

Roosevelt's speech captures a moment in time, and presumes that his listeners understand his reference to "existing diplomatic negotiations" as well as the inference that the efforts toward "the maintenance of peace in the Pacific" included an embargo on trade that had continued in the months leading up to the attack. Knowledge demand is further intensified by references to the diplomatic mechanisms of the government and the role of the secretary of state. Add to this the required knowledge about Oahu's geographic location relative to the mainland, and an understanding of the genre of speeches, which primarily persuade and inform, and you can begin to appreciate how this might challenge a high school student. The speech's fairly simple wording belies the complexity of the text itself.

Background Knowledge

We spoke in the previous chapter about the impact of students' lived experiences on their ability to comprehend texts. This can be especially challenging given the abstract nature of much of the content we teach. However, it isn't necessary for a student to walk on a volcano or witness a historical event for him or her to learn about Mount Vesuvius and its destruction of Pompeii. Instead, these experiences are bridged for the student through secondary experiences gained through media. Students today have access to all sorts of videos and online sources, and we all gain some background knowledge from those secondary experiences. While these secondary experiences are never absolute, they do build knowledge. Students in south Texas, for example, have a sense of snow because they see movies about blizzards and watch TV weather reports. That doesn't give them the true sense of cold and slipperiness of ice and snow that a student from a cold climate understands, and they can't have the sensory experience of heavy damp snow or light fluffy snow, but they do gain a working knowledge of the phenomenon.

These secondary experiences from media sources such as films, television shows, and online pictures and videos can provide support to readers as they encounter complex text. Readers may never have visited the Sahara or Mojave Deserts, but secondary experiences can allow them to develop a deeper understanding of the specialized topic of sand dunes in Gallant's (1997) *Sand on the Move: The Story of Dunes*.

Vocabulary

The ability to understand concepts is directly tied to an understanding of the vocabulary used to represent those concepts (RAND Reading Study Group, 2002). In fact, it is useful to think of vocabulary knowledge as a proxy for content knowledge. The way one explains the structure of an atomic particle is through the accurate use of terms like *neutron*, *electron*, and *proton*. Likewise, we persuade others about opposition to the Vietnam

War through the use of words like *protest, nonviolent resistance,* and *Summer of Love.* A troubling fact is that a significant number of students enter middle school without the necessary vocabulary to understand the content material they are reading. One study estimates that as many as 50 percent of sixth graders who are English learners are lacking this vocabulary (Lesaux & Kiefer, 2010). This presents challenges for the materials used in the classroom, reading and writing assignments, and even classroom discourse.

Academic vocabulary and academic language are two closely related factors for understanding the complexity of a text. The terms used to label concepts, processes, and objects are the academic vocabulary, and the words used to make these understandable to others are collectively the academic language. The devices used to link the terms together into a coherent set of ideas constitute the academic language, and include rhetorical devices used to explain and clarify. Without the academic language, the vocabulary would remain a static list of words with limited use.

Vacca and Vacca (2007) describe three kinds of vocabulary: general, specialized, and technical. This classification system allows teachers to determine which words in a text are worthy of being taught:

A troubling fact is that a significant number of students enter middle school without the necessary vocabulary to understand the content material they are reading.

- **General Vocabulary.** This category includes words that are widely used, highly frequent, and relatively easy to learn. General words comprise the bulk of students' speaking vocabulary.
- **Specialized Vocabulary.** This category focuses specifically on words that change meaning in different contexts or disciplines. For example, the word *expression* means one thing in general use yet something specific in mathematics. These words deserve specific attention from teachers, as students are likely to be confused by them.
- **Technical Vocabulary.** This category focuses on words that are discipline-specific. They are generally considered difficult words and occur much more rarely than general or specialized words. When evaluating a text, look for how these rare terms are discussed, as they may not require direct instruction if the author of the text is doing a good job of explaining the term, offering examples and nonexamples, and demonstrating how it is applied.

▶ Conclusion

Qualitative evaluation of informational text should always lead back to a consideration of the particular student user and to how he or she will use a given text. First, look for the conceptual density (the number of new concepts per unit of text) to ensure that there is not a significant overload of new information all at once. Second, see if the text introduces new content by making connections with what the reader already knows. Third, choose texts that include more information about fewer topics, rather than those that offer broad but shallow surveys of a topic. This will ensure that students are provided with a more precise focus on the content under investigation than they otherwise would be and, in turn, validate and extend the information students already have about a topic. Fourth, examine the text to see if it specifically addresses the common misconceptions readers have about the topic at hand. These misconceptions are often the source of audience and text mismatch, as students may not be able to integrate new information unless their misunderstandings are specifically addressed.

© Rachel Epstein/PhotoEdit

Exploring
Teacher-Led Tasks
Modeling Expert Thinking

I n selecting texts for classroom use, teachers need to consider more than
the quantitative and qualitative scores given to the reading. What students are expected to *do* with the text should also have an impact on the
selection. Simply put, when students are asked to read independently, the

selected texts have to be reasonably matched to their performance level. If teachers want students to read more complex texts, they have to teach them how to access these texts. Using high-quality instruction to increase the rigor of what students can read is the goal of teachers everywhere. The pathway for accessing complex texts requires that students encounter texts that are complex, learn to notice what is confusing, and then receive instruction in those areas of confusion. In other words, to increase rigor and complexity, the teacher has to share in the responsibility and do some of the work. Of course, students also have responsibility and must be engaged in the work. As we noted in Chapter 1, struggle is important. Efforts to remove all struggling can result in limited progress and development. Excessive struggle, however—especially without instruction—leads to frustration, resignation, and limited learning.

Struggle is important. Efforts to remove all struggling can result in limited progress and development. Excessive struggle, however, leads to frustration, resignation, and limited learning.

In the chapters that follow, we focus on a number of different tasks that teachers can use to ensure that students develop competence and confidence in reading. They include teacher-led, peer-led, and independent tasks. When the teacher is leading the task, the selected texts can be more complex. Teacher-led tasks are typically those in which the teacher is modeling his or her thinking. As apprentices, students need to have thinking made visible. In many ways, thinking is invisible, and the only way to illuminate it for students is to explicitly verbalize it. As Duffy (2003) noted, "The only way to model thinking is to talk about how to do it. That is, we provide a verbal description of the thinking one does or, more accurately, an *approximation* of the thinking involved" (p. 11).

Teacher modeling has been widely recognized as an effective tool for building students' proficiency and skill. Evidence of the benefits of this instructional practice can be found across teaching disciplines—from modeling to encourage food acceptance in preschool children (e.g., Hendy & Raudenbush, 2000), for example, to improving students' music performance (e.g., Haston, 2007). In the area of literacy, there is evidence that supports modeling in both reading and writing (e.g., Dunn, 2011; Fisher, Frey, & Lapp, 2011). As Allington and Cunningham (2007) note, "What all children need, and some need more of, is models, explanations, and demonstrations of how reading is accomplished" (p. 54).

In 2008(b), Fisher, Frey, and Lapp reported on an effort to observe twenty-five expert teachers' modeling practices. In order of frequency, these were the skills most commonly modeled for students:

- **Comprehension Skills**—focused on modeling how cognitive processes such as inferring, visualizing, making connections, predicting, summarizing, monitoring, clarifying, and questioning can be used to make sense of a text
- **Word-Solving Skills**—focused on modeling how the meaning of unknown words can be determined through the use of context clues, word parts, and other outside resources, such as online reference tools or consultation with a peer
- **Text Structure Analysis Skills**—focused on modeling how to organize thinking about the ways in which an author structured a text, ranging from macro-level considerations (narrative versus expository) to more discrete-level concerns (problem/solution, cause/effect, and sequence)
- **Text Feature Analysis Skills**—focused on modeling how visual and graphic tools that are added to a text, such as illustrations, diagrams, charts, figures, captions, bold words, headings, margin notes, and the like, aid in our understanding of a text

In 2011, we provided extensive coaching to eight middle school teachers to help them integrate modeling into their instructional practices. These teachers taught a total of 446 students. We then compared the academic performance of these students with that of the students who were *not* enrolled in any classes with the teachers who had received coaching. The results were impressive: there were significant gains in student achievement when teachers modeled—on a daily basis—their thinking about reading.

In both of these studies, teachers modeled with texts they had selected based on their students' instructional needs and the content under investigation. For example, if students were working on writing informational texts, the teacher might have modeled using texts with various structures so that students could experience different examples of the thinking that was behind each type. Since these studies were conducted, there has been an increased focus on cultivating disciplinary literacy, which is another area in which teachers can model. In addition, teachers can model their understanding of factors of text complexity, which is a broad category that encompasses the notion of text structure and text feature analysis that we previously discussed. The four overarching areas in which teachers can model with complex texts are comprehension, word solving, disciplinary literacy, and factors of complexity.

▶ Comprehension

In terms of comprehension, teachers can model the use of cognitive strategies such as visualizing, inferring, summarizing, predicting, questioning, or monitoring. Importantly, these cognitive strategies should be used when appropriate based on clues from the text. They should not be curricularized, with four weeks devoted to summarizing, for example, and then the next four weeks devoted to predicting. Readers have to learn to notice the text clues that trigger specific, useful cognitive strategies. Just as important, students need to see that these are ultimately problem-solving approaches to be used when meaning breaks down.

Readers have to learn to notice the text clues that trigger specific, useful cognitive strategies. Just as important, students need to see that these are ultimately problem-solving approaches to be used when meaning breaks down.

Comprehension strategies alone often cannot compensate when texts are complex. Take, for example, the following sentence from a glossary: *Somites are blocks of mesodermal cells adjacent to the notochord during vertebrate organogenesis.* Unless the reader has sufficient prior knowledge and related vocabulary understanding, predicting or visualizing is not likely to be of use. That's not to say that modeling comprehension is futile, however. Readers still deploy a range of cognitive moves as they read texts—they just have to notice when these are working and when they are not working, and then know what to do about it when their comprehension has been compromised. This is how students progress from being strategic readers to being skilled ones (Afflerbach, Pearson, & Paris, 2008).

To make the most of comprehension strategies such as making predictions, visualizing information, determining importance, and so on, it is important to explicitly label the strategy and the factors that make the text complex. For example, sixth-grade teacher Maureen Sheehan models informational text from the first chapter of a book. She first reads the following sentences:

> Phineas Gage's accident will make him world famous, but fame will do him little good. Yet for many others— psychologists, medical researchers, doctors, and especially those who suffer brain injuries—Phineas Gage will become someone worth knowing. (Fleischman, 2002, p. 2)

She then thinks aloud:

> As I reread those last two sentences, I began forming a prediction about the text. The writer is using opposite ideas by saying Phineas will be world famous but it will not do any good for him. I believe the author wrote that statement to get me wondering and curious. I'm thinking, "What do you mean by such an odd statement?" But he doesn't answer my question. Instead, he says that other professionals, and people with brain injuries, will know about Phineas. The writer isn't ready for me to fully understand this yet, but he wants me to know what's coming. The writer wrote these sentences so that I would make a prediction about what he will be explaining later in the book.

In labeling the comprehension strategy (predicting), she alerts her students to her cognitive interaction with the text based on what she has read to this point. She then strengthens it further by linking it to the author's craft of using a provocative statement—one that is designed to elicit a predictive response in the reader that will be satisfied later.

▶ Word Solving

Modeling word solving remains a staple of effective instructional practice, and is probably even more important in the context of complex texts. During the modeling of word solving, the point is not to teach individual words and phrases or simply to tell students what words mean, but rather to help students develop their own habits when it comes to resolving unknown words. The goal of modeling word (and phrase) solving is to help students develop a habit of looking inside words and outside words to get an idea of what the words might mean. Looking inside the word involves investigating word parts, including prefixes, suffixes, roots, bases, and cognates. Looking outside the word involves the exploration of context clues and resources. Of course, word solving does not always work, and teachers should model scenarios in which these systems fail as well the more ideal cases in which they work.

For example, first-grade teacher Alexandria Nieto models how she figures out the word *pod* in *Baby Dolphin's First Day* (Roop & Roop, 2011).

I'm not sure that I understand what the author means by *pod*. It says, "Their group is called a pod" [p. 19]. I'm thinking, "What group is called a pod?" I'm not sure that I have heard that word before. I think I'll read the page before. It says, "Dolphins swim together" [p. 18]. Oh, so I think that a pod means a group of dolphins because I see them swimming together in the picture, and a group of them is called a pod. I think I'll read the next page. It says, "The pod swims fast" [p. 20], and the picture shows a group of dolphins. I think I'm right—the author helped me to understand that *pod* is the name for a group of dolphins.

▶ Disciplinary Thinking

Modeling with complex texts often provides teachers with an opportunity to explore the discipline from which a given text was drawn and, on the flip side, to examine the text for traces of its connection to the associated discipline. Science texts differ from historical texts—not to mention the many nuances inherent in literary texts. As students get older, certainly as they reach the upper elementary grade levels, they should experience thinking that aligns with the discipline under investigation. As Shanahan and Shanahan (2014) note, students who continue to read informational texts of increasing complexity as if they were stories will not succeed. Modeling is the vehicle through which this experience of thinking like a disciplinary expert can come alive for students. As teachers model the habits of a reader in a specific discipline, they help prepare students to access increasingly complex texts.

Figure 5.1 contains some general ideas about the differences between texts from three disciplines. Of course, readers can do all of these things in just about any text, but experts in these disciplines tend to do some things more than those in other fields.

For example, while modeling using excepts from First Lady Dolley Madison's 1814 letter to her sister on the burning of Washington, fifth-grade teacher Hal Dickinson reads aloud through the text in its entirety so his students will understand the general meaning, then returns to several points:

> When I read this document, the first thing I look for is who wrote it, when, and to whom. I can see that Dolley Madison wrote it to her sister, so I am expecting that this is going to be a personal communication, not a formal report.

Figure 5.1 Aspects of Disciplinary Literacy

Reading Like a Scientist	Reading Like a Historian	Reading Literature
• **Writer's Expertise.** Is the writer credible? • **Evidence.** What evidence does the author furnish to support claims? • **Classifying.** How does this information fit with models I already know? • **Questions.** What questions does this text raise? • **Investigation.** Where can I obtain more information?	• **Sourcing.** Analyze who produced the document and use that information to analyze the viewpoint and reliability of the document. • **Contextualizing.** Consider the document in historical context including when it was written, where, and what else was happening at the time. • **Corroborating.** Read across multiple documents to identify points of agreement and disagreement.	• **Author Craft.** Analyze the choices an author made, including genre, narrator, and literary devices. • **Contextualizing.** Consider the text in its social and historical context including when it was written, where, and what else was happening at the time. • **Theme.** Determine the underlying message or "big idea" that indicates the author's belief about life. Readers consider a given text against universal themes that transcend culture and language to explore the human experience.

In doing so, he is modeling for his students how historians source information to gain a sense of its veracity.

Mr. Dickinson next draws their attention to a passage that explains that the narrator's friend was angry:

> I insist on waiting until the large picture of General Washington is secured, and it requires to be unscrewed from the wall. This process was found too tedious for these perilous moments; I have ordered the frame to be broken, and the canvas taken out. It is done! and the precious portrait placed in the hands of two gentlemen of New York, for safe keeping. (Madison, 1814)

He then models his thinking about the passage: "One of the things historians do is look for corroborating evidence. I remember that we read about this in our social studies book. Let's find the page where it told us this story."

As his students locate the page, several begin to raise their hands. "Here it is, Mr. Dickinson," they say. "It's on page 127! The picture's there, too!"

▶ Factors of Complexity

Modeling requires that teachers analyze the text they plan to use. In some cases, the text is complex in areas other than those previously mentioned, and modeling comprehension strategies or word-solving skills will not result in deep understanding for students. In these cases, teachers may model for students examples of the factors of complexity that contribute to the complexity of a given text. This category of modeling is vast in nature, given the various ways that texts can be complex.

When a text is complex in the area of narration, the teacher should model his or her thinking about the narrator and how the teacher knows what the narrator is doing. When a text is complex in the area of genre, the teacher can model his or her understanding of the characteristics of the given genre. Importantly, making predictions or visualizing may not help a reader understand a text that is complex in other nonrelated ways. It's hard to visualize appropriately, for instance, if the narrator is misleading or if the various narrators have different perspectives. It's hard to make an accurate prediction if text features such as charts and diagrams are not understood.

It's Snowing (Gibbons, 2011) is an interesting informational text for second-grade students. A cursory review of this text reveals that it is complex in several areas: in its density of information, in its text features, in its reliance on the reader's background knowledge, and in its apparent lack of a clear purpose. Recognizing these factors of complexity should guide the instruction students receive. Of course, this book could be used for a close reading lesson. During close reading, students use what they have been taught to analyze a text collaboratively with peers. Close reading lessons rely on students' ability to analyze texts at increasingly complex levels. The way that they learn to do this is by participating in modeling and practice.

As with each category of modeling, there are likely more areas that could potentially be modeled than students actually need or that teachers even have the time for. If we return to *It's Snowing*, for example, we see that second-grade teacher Natalie Hanson decides to focus her modeling on the text features found in the book. We discussed the various types of text features in Chapters 3 and 4, but did not comment on the ways in which students can learn to use these text features on their own. When teachers model their thinking about these features and the ways in which they use them while they are reading, students learn to apply the approach to new and increasingly complex texts. For example, when referring students to page 5, Ms. Hanson says,

> I see a small box off to the side with some text inside it. I bet that will be a caption because I know that authors sometimes add information to help the reader make sense of an image or illustration. I like to read any captions that I find first because I don't want to be confused by the text or pictures, which can happen, and it's why authors add those captions.

Later in the text, on pages 14 and 15, Ms. Hanson also models her understanding of the text features, saying,

> These pages look like a grid to me because of the white spaces between all of the pictures. I see the names of six of the continents, and I remember from the previous page that the author said that it snows on all seven continents. I expect that these pages will include information about snow for each continent.

Teachers shouldn't model only one aspect of text complexity throughout an entire text, however, as was the case in the previous two examples. Rather, wise teachers know that they should start with an analysis of the factors of complexity and then identify the areas in which their students need instruction. Just because a text is complex in a given area does not mean that students, at a given grade or a given point in the school year or unit of study, need instruction on that aspect.

Toward the end of the lesson on *It's Snowing*, Ms. Hanson thinks aloud:

> I'm wondering about the purpose of this text. The author doesn't really tell me. I'm going to go back and take another look at this to see what I think about the purpose. On these first few pages *[flipping through pages 1 to 4]*, I was thinking that this was going to be a story. I see lots of illustrations of kids, and they're playing outside when it starts to snow. Then the text changes, and the author gives me information about snow and

how it forms. Then there are these pages about snow in
different places. I'm thinking that the author is providing
me with accurate information, helping me understand
different facts about the snow. I think this is an
informational text because it has descriptions and facts
that I can check. It informs me about snow. I am going
to keep this book as a reference for when I need to write
an informational report. I think it is a good example of a
report that I could use.

Teachers can also model their thinking about the use of different structures in a given text to demonstrate how they use those structures to
understand the text and predict what the author will do next. For example, when the author provides a cause for something such as the Great
Depression, teachers can explain to students that the reader should then
expect an effect to follow. Similarly, when the author introduces a problem, teachers can explain to students that this signals the reader to understand that a solution is likely forthcoming. In terms of narrative texts,
teachers can model the ways in which literary devices help them understand the text.

For example, while reading *Click, Clack, Moo: Cows That Type* (Cronin,
2000) with first graders, the teacher, Angie Lopez, first notes that structure
helps her understand that the book is fictional:

I'm seeing on this first page that the cows are typing.
I know that cows don't really type, so I think that this
is probably fiction. I know that authors sometimes
use animals that talk to make a point and teach me
something. I'll read on and see what that is.

In addition to modeling the ways in which the use of literary devices
impacts their thinking, teachers can model their understanding of story
grammar. As we discussed in Chapter 3, most literary texts follow a consistent narrative structure, which can be characterized as story grammar.
Later in her lesson on the book about typing cows, the teacher models her
thinking about this structure:

I think that this is our conflict. I remember that the cows
wrote a letter to the farmer asking for electric blankets

because the barn was closed. Now, they are on strike, and the sign says, "No milk today." I expect that the farmer will be very unhappy and this conflict will have to be resolved.

Over time, with the use of modeling strategies like these, students will learn to analyze the overall factors of complexity of texts as well as the more specific structures of those texts, investigating how specific sentences, paragraphs, and larger portions of the text relate to each other and to the whole.

▶ Key Components of Modeling

Our experience suggests that there are two teacher behaviors that are critical in the area of modeling. The first is the use of "I" statements. When teachers use "I" statements, they alert listeners to the internal process of the speaker. They also invite the learner into the speaker's thinking and do not suggest that *you*, the student, should be doing something other than observing and analyzing the thinking of an expert who is reading. The teachers profiled in this chapter used "I" statements with their students, which allowed them to personalize their thinking and imply that there are likely other ways to think about a given text.

The second behavior critical in the area of modeling is the teacher's verbalization of the metacognitive strategies that inform his or her thinking. When modeling, students deserve to hear the *because*, *why*, or *how* of the thinking. If they only hear the example of the thinking, even using an "I" statement, they are likely to have a good idea about what the teacher is thinking, but not about how the teacher came to that understanding. In other words, teachers need to provide students the examples and the thinking *behind the examples* so that they can develop the habit that the teacher is modeling.

Figure 5.2 is a planning tool for modeling that contains much more than these two basic ideas. Importantly, not all texts require a teacher to take all of the steps described. We included all of them, however, to highlight the various ways in which teachers can use modeling to provide students with instruction in complex texts. For example, while reading *From the Mixed-Up Files of Mrs. Basil E. Frankweiler* (Konigsburg, 1967), fourth-grade teacher Amber Cruise stops after reading a section about looking for fingerprints

Figure 5.2 Design a Think-Aloud

Examples: Possible Features to Model	Your Text: Features You Plan to Model
1. **Name the strategy, skill, or task.** "As I read this text, I'm thinking about the organizational system the author used."	
2. **State the purpose of the strategy, skill, or task.** "When I figure out the organization, I can better follow what the author is trying to tell me, and it helps me anticipate what the author will do next."	
3. **Explain when the strategy or skill is used.** "I often use this approach when I start to read an informational text to see if there is a structure or organization that I'm familiar with. If there is, I can also use my knowledge of the organization to take notes."	
4. **Use analogies to link prior knowledge to new learning.** "I think of organization like a map that helps me get to my destination, which is making sure that I understand the information and then how I can use it."	
5. **Demonstrate how the skill, strategy, or task is completed.** "I've just read the first two paragraphs, and I can tell that there is a problem. The author doesn't use that word, but he doesn't have to. I recognize the problem because he has said that people were worried."	
6. **Alert learners to errors to avoid.** "I have to be careful not to jump to conclusions too fast and to watch out because authors can use many different organizational systems in a text and can switch along the way. For now, I know it's a problem, so I can write the problem in my notes and I am ready for the solution."	
7. **Assess the use of the skill.** "Now, I've read three more paragraphs, and the solution was there. I know that because the author said that it calmed people down. This is working for me as I take my notes so that I'm ready to talk about this text with my team."	

on a statue that might have been made by Michelangelo. The text reads as follows:

> Jamie snapped his fingers. "I've got it!" he exclaimed. He held up his hands for Claudia to see.
> "What does that mean?"
> "Fingerprints, silly. If Michelangelo worked on this statue, his fingerprints could be on it." (pp. 62–63)

The teacher adds,

> I was trying to visualize this in my mind. I can see Michelangelo working on the statue and getting his fingerprints all over it. But I'm thinking about something else. If Michelangelo made the statue, it would be really old because he lived in the 1500s. And I wonder if the fingerprints would still be on the statue after all of those years. I also wonder if anyone saved Michelangelo's fingerprints. If there were fingerprints on the statue, and no one had Michelangelo's fingerprints, then this wouldn't work. I think that there are too many complications for this to actually prove the statue was created by Michelangelo. I predict that they're going to have to find another way to figure this out. I keep thinking about the title of the book and wondering if there is better information about the statue in those mixed-up files because we haven't heard much about the files yet, and the author did put that in the title.

Sometimes, it is appropriate for students to meet a complex text first, and then hear their teacher's thinking about the text. Other times, teacher modeling occurs as the students see the text for the first time.

Figure 5.3 includes a sample of teacher modeling with older students that focuses on informational text. Maria Lawson, the ninth-grade science teacher profiled in the figure, asks her students to read the text first and notice what is confusing. In many situations, it is appropriate for students to meet a complex text first, identify what caused them difficulty, and then hear their teacher's thinking about the text. At other times, as in Ms. Cruz's classroom, teacher modeling occurs as the students see the text for the first time. These instructional decisions are made, in part, based on the demand of the text and the skills of the students.

Figure 5.3   Sample Teacher Modeling

Text	Teacher Commentary During the Think-Aloud	Strategies Modeled/Practiced
Going Through Changes (Photo of pancakes)	"As I look over this piece of text, I see a photo of pancakes cooking on a griddle. Some are golden brown, and others are still a beige batter color. The title of this reading is *Going Through Changes*. I wonder if the pancakes, some uncooked and others fully done, represent changes at a chemical level. I'll read the first paragraph."	Predicting and using titles and graphics provides focus and motivation to read further.
At a dinner table, a cook is making pancakes. He mixes together an egg, milk, and flour into a batter. When the batter is placed on the griddle, it becomes solid and golden brown. The batter has had a chemical change. All the atoms of the original ingredients are still in the batter. But the griddle's heat has arranged those atoms in a different pattern. Like the pancake batter, many substances go through chemical changes. These changes can break down complex substances into simpler parts. Or they can join simple parts into complex substances.	"So the cooking batter does represent chemical changes. I see from reading these paragraphs that chemical changes involve substances breaking down and substances joining together. "I think the next section will tell me about how this process of breaking down and building up occurs. Do you have any ideas?" Maria listens as the students share a few possibilities. Janette, a student in Maria's class, responds, "Maybe the next section will talk about molecules being broken down or atoms being joined together." "Yes," Dave says. "I remember when I was in eighth grade we talked about how salt molecules are broken down when salt is added to water." "OK," Maria continues, "let's read on to see if we're correct."	The prediction is confirmed by reading the text. Note that sometimes the prediction is refuted after reading the text. Afterward, the main ideas are identified by summarizing a few lines of the text, which is followed by another prediction based on the text just read.

Text	Teacher Commentary During the Think-Aloud	Strategies Modeled/Practiced
It usually takes energy to combine substances in a chemical reaction. This kind of reaction is called an endothermic reaction.	"An *endothermic reaction*. Wow, I'm not sure what that means, but I do know that *thermic* sounds like a word part from *thermometer* or *thermal* and both of those terms relate to heat. "Maybe *endothermic* also relates to heat in some way. I'll continue to read. Maybe I'll gain an understanding of the meaning of this word if I read on."	Segmenting words into word parts brings attention to root words or affixes that might offer clues to meaning. In addition, it provides students with an understanding that clarification might come from context or from continued reading.
For example, heat was needed to turn the batter into a pancake.	"I guess I was right— *endothermic* does relate to heat."	Again, a prediction, in this case a prediction about a word's meaning, may be confirmed or refuted by reading upcoming text.
If iron and powdered sulfur were mixed together, nothing would happen. But apply heat to those combined substances, and you would form iron sulfide. This is an entirely new substance.	"So heat added to a mixture can cause a new substance to form. Interesting. Maybe *endothermic* means that heat is added."	Synthesizes and restates— examples offered in the text can help the reader to infer word meaning.

Source: Lapp, Fisher, & Grant (2008).

▶ A Modeling Caution

While modeling, the teacher is doing most of the work. That doesn't mean that students sit idly by as the teacher shares his or her thinking. Instead, students should be thinking along. They should be anticipating what the teacher will do, and the teacher should pause periodically to encourage students to try on what they have experienced by talking with a partner. For example, when fourth-grade teacher Joe Bradley hypothetically asks several questions of an author that are of interest to him, he invites students to turn to a partner and ask their own questions of the author. Similarly, when kindergarten teacher Misty Stevens indicates that she thinks the text she is reading is fiction because she doesn't know of cats that talk, she invites students to turn to a partner and identify other aspects of the text that might suggest it is fiction as well.

▶ Conclusion

Modeling has long held an important role in developing students' literacy. Even so, student encounters with complex text call for teachers to update their modeling behaviors; an analysis of the factors that make a given text complex and—for students in upper elementary and secondary grades—an exploration of any related disciplinary literacy considerations are key to ensuring success with this practice. Together with a continued focus on modeling word solving and building students' analytic skills, teachers should consider the ways in which comprehension strategies can be used to guide students' thinking. In turn, students should learn these comprehension skills, but also recognize that they may not be as effective in complex texts as they are in more comfortable texts. In short, when we add modeling to our repertoire of instructional habits, students will have a much better chance of accessing complex texts than they otherwise would.

© Robert W. Ginn/PhotoEdit

Exploring
Teacher-Led Tasks
Closely Reading Complex Texts

Since the first edition of this book, significant attention has been focused on close reading. This approach to text analysis involves a reader returning to a given text more than once to analyze the language, structures, and patterns as a means to become informed about the message being shared. Close reading isn't a teaching strategy in and of itself. Rather, it is an approach to reading. Close reading involves the myriad ways in which proficient readers make sense of complex text—all with the end goal of understanding what the author is doing and accomplishing, and what the information means. More specifically, close reading involves students identifying a purpose(s) for reading, accessing and using prior knowledge, analyzing and determining the meaning of discipline- or topic-based language, organizing and interpreting information, and refining and revising their understanding during each rereading.

Close reading as an approach to text analysis has quite a long history. Referred to as *exegesis* by early Greek scholars, close reading was the interpretative approach used to interrogate sacred texts (Juel, 1998). The idea of close text analysis surfaced again in 1929, when Richards gave his students poems and did not tell them who wrote them or when they were written. He wanted his students to concentrate on the words on the page and to derive the correct meaning from the words themselves, with no preconceived notions about the text or influences from their own lives. This insular view of text interpretation resulted in the *New Criticism* movement that was developed around 1930 by Empson, a student of Richards.

Over the years, close reading has fallen in and out of favor. When the pendulum swung *away* from the focus on the text itself, as noted by Blau (1994), more importance was placed on a reader's interpretation of the text: "A work of literature is an inert text that can hardly be said to have more than a potential for meaning until it is called into being by a reader who constructs a reading, thereby giving meaning to the text" (p. 26). Rosenblatt (1995) then called for a more balanced approach, noting in her discussion of reader response theory that "[t]he reader must remain faithful to the author's text and must be alert to the potential clues concerning character and motive" (p. 11). Rosenblatt was concerned that readers might ignore elements in a text and fail to realize that they were "imputing to the author views unjustified by the text" (p. 11). Her concerns were valid with respect to the way the reader response approach was sometimes overemphasized in the classroom: too often students were encouraged to make text-to-self connections to share *somewhat* related personal experiences, but teachers then failed to have them juxtapose these against the text itself. In these scenarios, classmates may have responded by adding additional personal experiences, and the discussion often ended before they returned to the text. The lack of *returning* to the text, rather than the making of irrelevant connections, was the point of concern. As Pearson (2013) noted, there is always an inherent balancing act at play—and also an inextricable link—between a reader's consideration of his or her experiences as they relate to a text and his or her quest to determine the meaning of the text: "We use our knowledge of the world, along with our knowledge of how language and texts work, to make all the local inferences required to connect the sentences to one another—to build a coherent representation of what the text says" (p. 16).

To ensure that close reading becomes an approach used by every reader, teachers need to

- Model what close reading looks like in each discipline
- Explain the power of close textual analysis
- Design instruction that invites readers to consider the sociopolitical and historical contexts of the text while also focusing on what the author actually said
- Support all students with the appropriate scaffolds to analyze the meaning of the text, encouraging them to think deeply about what is being said and about the language and structures the author used to share the information
- Encourage students to refine, transfer, and generate new knowledge

▶ Key Features of Close Reading Lessons

There are a number of characteristics that mark a close reading lesson— namely that students are reading (and rereading) a short, worthy piece of text; marking the text in some way; discussing the text with peers; and considering questions that require evidence from the text.

Selecting Short, Worthy Passages

It's wise to use a short piece of text because to really understand a text, the reader will likely have to read it more than once. Long pieces of text make it hard for students to reread within the context of the classroom. We aren't suggesting that students should read only short pieces of text. They can read a subsection of a science or social studies text or sections of a novel being read by the whole class. When readers read to really understand something, whether it's literary or informational text, they need to read closely enough to make sense of what the author is saying and to then compare that with other topically related texts and their own experiences and beliefs.

For example, Amy Donovan selected John Boyce's (2006) novel *Boy in the Striped Pajamas* to share with her eighth graders. This 216-page fictional text set in Nazi Germany tells the story of two unlikely friends. Although Ms. Donovan knew that stand-alone texts could be used for close reading, she wanted her students to realize that readers linger over certain passages within a novel to glean a deeper meaning.

Some sections of the novel were read aloud by Ms. Donovan to model her thinking for her students, and much of the book was discussed during peer-led collaborative tasks. The students also engaged in several close readings throughout the text. The passages the teacher identified as candidates for this level of attention were ones needing deeper analysis because of their complexity. One section the teacher believed would challenge her students appears in Chapter 5 when Bruno and his father talk about their new home. Ms. Donovan was sure that without a close look at the dialogue between the two characters, her students would not understand the complex relationship between them. The conversation in question is more than a disagreement between a father and son, and Ms. Donovan wanted her students to see the indirect characterizations in the exchange so that they would have a foundation to better understand the two through events that occur later in the text.

Ms. Donovan asked the students to read the selected pages and to pay close attention to the author's use of language to develop a profile of Bruno's dad. Through partner and class discussions that were fueled with references to the text and to their annotations, the students concluded that two of the father's main characteristics are that he is undemonstrative and loyal. The following exchange shows how Ms. Donovan's questions and probes about the text supported a deeper understanding:

Ms. Donovan:	What's the relationship like between Bruno and his father?
Alberto:	Kind of the same as me and my dad.
Ms. Donovan:	Okay, but what words in the text tell you about that relationship? What language does the author use?
Alberto:	Well, Bruno is shouting at his dad.

Jason:	Yeah, but his dad's using a quiet voice. I don't think Bruno's dad shows much emotion.
Baylee:	You don't? What does it say that makes you think so?
Jason:	It says that "nothing could make father angry today," and Bruno says that his father "rarely became angry."
Alberto:	Oh, I see. And here it says that "he became quiet and distant." Also, it says he is "staring at his stony face." That'd be like a statue.
Ms. Donovan:	What words in the text help you understand their relationship?
Michael:	It seems like he's loyal to his family.
Ms. Donavan:	How do you know that?
Amal:	Yeah, and to his country. It says here [pointing] that "this is my work, important work. Important to our country. Important to the Führer."
Luis:	So, like, he's a loyal person, and his family and his country are important to him.

During this exchange, students were beginning to piece together the kind of relationship Bruno and his father have. They went deeper than understanding that the father and son are having a disagreement to uncover some of the more veiled qualities that could be used to describe their relationship.

Rereading

It isn't uncommon for students to read a passage once, read it quickly and rather superficially, and then announce, "I'm done!" Sophisticated readers understand that the nature of some texts requires that they be read more than once. Even with less dense text, it is essential to glean the details at both the explicit and implicit levels in order to fully understand the reading. Close reading requires a willingness to return to the text to read part of it—or even all of it—more than once.

The texts selected for close reading are not likely to give up their deeper meaning easily or quickly. Thus, regardless of grade level, students should be expected to reread the text as part of a close reading lesson. In the primary grades, students may or may not do this independently. In some cases, the teacher is the person who rereads while students identify evidence.

In other cases, students in the primary grades read sections of the text to locate the information they're looking for. Both of these scenarios played out while a group of kindergarten students were reading *The Day the Crayons Quit* (Daywalt, 2013). Anton asked his teacher to reread the letter from Blue Crayon so that his group could identify the problem that Blue Crayon needs to have solved. Another group was studying the final picture in which Duncan, the boy who receives the letters from the crayons, responds to their complaints. They analyzed each image to determine whether or not Duncan has responded appropriately.

In the upper grades, students are most commonly the ones doing the rereading. That isn't to say that the teacher wouldn't read the text aloud, perhaps at the third reading, to facilitate students' understanding. This is especially common when the text is a speech, when it contains dialogue, or in cases where it may be a recording of the author. For example, a group of fifth graders were able to hear Langston Hughes read "The Negro Speaks of Rivers" after having read and studied the poem several times (awetblackbough, 2010).

In addition, students in the upper grades are often asked to read the text to their peers in small groups. Importantly, this is done not cold, on the first reading of the text, but rather after several readings. For example, as part of the close reading of Chief Joseph's "I Will Fight No More Forever" speech, groups of fifth-grade students asked members of their group to read the text aloud. The point is that students across the grade levels have multiple interactions with the same text. Additional examples of the differences between close reading in Grades K–2 versus Grades 3–12 can be found in Figure 6.1.

Reading With a Pencil

Close reading requires reading with a pencil—well, perhaps not literally a pencil, but some note-taking device. As readers, most of us want to write in or on the text. We make margin notes, we highlight, we underline—all because the act of making notes helps us pay attention to the text and allows us to return to it later when we want to provide evidence. But writing in books in school is frowned upon, so we have to teach students other ways to "read with a pencil." This might include asking students to take traditional notes on lined paper, to use interactive graphic organizers, or to compose digital notes. The actual system of note taking is less important than the overall necessity of taking notes during close reading.

The annotations in a book reveal much about the reader. Edgar Allan Poe (1844/1988), himself an unapologetic penciler, wrote, "in the marginalia,

Figure 6.1   Comparing Close Reading in Primary and Upper Grades

Close Reading in Primary Grades	Elements	Close Reading in Upper Grades
The reading level of the text is significantly higher than students' reading level.	Text Selection	The text complexity is slightly higher than what the student takes on during other phases of reading instruction.
The teacher is reading the text aloud to students, although they are not grasping its deeper meaning. The text may or may not be displayed.	Initial Reading	Students are more likely to read the text independently, although they are not fully grasping its deeper meaning.
The teacher guides annotation practices using displayed text and fosters collaboratively developed annotations.	Annotation	Students familiar with annotation practices are marking the text independently and adding to their annotations throughout class discussions.
The teacher reads the text aloud multiple times. Students may read along at the paragraph, sentence, phrase, or individual word level. A few students may read the text independently in subsequent readings due to practice effects.	Repeated Readings	Students are rereading independently or with minimal support. Students may also have access to audio supports (a poet reading her poem, a teacher reading dialogue, a peer reading a key sentence).
Text-Based Discussions Students engage in extended discussion, which is driven by text-dependent questions and dialogic teaching. Students deepen their understanding through analysis of the literal, structural, and inferential dimensions of the text.		
Students draw and write collaboratively and independently, with adult support and guidance. They engage in shared investigations and debate compelling questions.	Responding to Texts	Students write collaboratively and independently. They investigate and research, and debate compelling questions.

too, we talk only to ourselves; we therefore talk freshly—boldly—originally—with abandonment—without conceit" (p. 7). Making notes to oneself during a reading was for centuries a widespread practice, but fell out of favor in the

20th century as public libraries became common. To write in a book was thought to sully it somehow. To be sure, writing in a text that doesn't belong to you isn't looked upon kindly. But in the process of protecting public books, we sometimes have a tendency to forget about the gains to be had from writing in the ones that belong to us alone.

In their seminal text, *How to Read a Book* (1972), Adler and Van Doren laid out a case for engaging in repeated readings with accompanying annotation:

> Why is marking a book indispensable to reading it? First, it keeps you awake—not merely conscious, but wide awake. Second, reading, if active, is thinking, and thinking tends to express itself in words, spoken or written. The person who says he knows what he thinks but cannot express it usually does not know what he thinks. Third, writing your reactions down helps you remember the thoughts of the author. (p. 49)

They then went on to describe the most common annotation marks:

- **Underlining** for major points
- **Vertical lines in the margin** to denote longer statements that are too long to be underlined
- **Stars, asterisks, or other doodads in the margin** to be used sparingly to emphasize the ten or dozen most important statements (*Note:* When using this type of annotation, you may want to fold a corner of each page where you make such a mark or place a slip of paper between the pages.)
- **Numbers in the margin** to indicate a sequence of points made by the author in development of an argument
- **Numbers of other pages in the margin** to indicate where else in the book the author makes the same points
- **Circling of key words or phrases** to serve much the same function as underlining
- **Writing in the margin or at the top or bottom of the page** to record questions (and perhaps answers) that a passage raises in your mind (Adler & Van Doren, 1940/1972, pp. 49–50)

Eleventh-grade English teacher Marcus Boulanger asked his students to annotate text as they read. Many of his students were good readers, but they had what Mr. Boulanger called a "naïve understanding" of their ability to hold extensive amounts of information in their minds. "Some of them think that reading is reading, whether it's a novel you're reading at the beach or a scientific paper about an experiment," he said.

Mr. Boulanger introduced his students to a method of annotation similar to the one described by Adler and Van Doren at the beginning of the school year, and his students now use this method when engaged in close readings. After the class had read the short story "Sonny's Blues" (Baldwin, 1965) for the first time, they returned to the reading, this time examining it more closely for themes. Mr. Boulanger had created a copy of the text with a column for annotated notes on the left side of the pages so that students could write on the text. At his direction, they combed the reading to find examples of Baldwin's use of darkness and light as a way to contrast the relationship between the two brothers. The students then discussed this imagery in their table groups:

By annotating literary and informational texts, students learn to slow down their reading to mine the depths of the concepts, arguments, and metaphors used by the writer.

Khadijah:	I underlined right here where he said "the bright sun deadened his dark brown damp skin" because I could imagine how sickly Sonny must have looked in the outside light.
Pablo:	That's good. Yeah, you're right. I wrote a note to myself about him bein' in the club, and there were jazz musicians. I was thinking 'bout there being a piano there, and the keys are black and white . . .
Elisa:	And you play different notes, like some are sharp and some are flat.
Khadijah:	Sounds like those piano lessons finally paid off for you.
Elisa:	[laughs] Yeah, but it's true. I marked this part where the narrator is talking about when the old folks are all together and it's just starting to get dark . . .
Pablo:	Yeah, and the kid is scared that things will change, and then it says . . . wait, I circled it right here . . .

Elisa:	I got it. "And when the light fills the room, the child is filled with darkness. He knows that every time this happens, he's moved just a little closer to the darkness outside."
Khadijah:	It's like that poem we read, about "Nothing gold can stay" [Frost, 1923/2011]. You're a little kid, but you're growing up, and you know that feeling safe and protected is going to go away.

By annotating literary and informational texts, students learn to slow down their reading to mine the depths of the concepts, arguments, and metaphors used by the writer. While this practice isn't necessary—or even desirable—for everything students read, it is important when the information in the text requires close inspection to unlock its meaning.

Discussing the Text

Collaborative conversations allow students to engage in purposeful talk, manage their use of academic and domain-specific language and concepts, and provide an opportunity for them to learn about themselves, each other, and the world. Students should be able to

- Engage in a variety of grade-level topical conversations in small- and large-group settings with a diverse range of learners
- Prepare for the discussion (e.g., complete the related reading in advance)
- Follow discussion guidelines and purposes, including specified assigned roles
- Ask and answer questions, request clarification, furnish evidence and examples, and contribute ideas that enhance the discussion
- Summarize and synthesize a speaker's main points

We devote an entire chapter of this book to collaborative conversations but wanted to mention it here because we believe that close reading requires this type of peer support and mediation. In addition to understanding the routines and procedures we share in Chapter 8, it's important to note that the questions students and teachers share about the text are critical because they provide fodder for the conversations students need to have.

▶ Text-Dependent Questions Scaffold Student Thinking

Questions form the core of discussion, and wise teachers come to the conversation equipped with queries designed to spur thinking. However, the analytical thinking one hopes for doesn't happen right out of the gate. Chances are good that there will be some struggle involved, but text-dependent questions that are well crafted can lead students on a path toward thinking critically. Questions that move the conversation from literal to interpretive stances assist students in deepening their comprehension. This path to comprehension is divided into three phases (Fisher, Frey, Anderson, & Thayre, 2014, p. 14):

- What does the text *say*? (literal meaning)
- How does the text *work*? (structural analysis)
- What does the text *mean*? (inferential and critical thinking)

Text-dependent questions cause students to reread a text in order to locate answers. This is rereading for a purpose, not for compliance. However, text-dependent questions aren't trivial, focused on the minutiae of the piece. In fact, even those at the literal level should be aligned to the major points the text holds. Like any successful journey, the quest toward comprehension is dependent on navigating the trek with a destination in mind. As the teacher, you're the guide, and your questions should point your students in the right direction, without too many side trips that delay the arrival. In the upcoming sections, we will describe each of these phases across two classroom settings. The first setting is a third-grade classroom where the teacher leads a close reading of a passage from a biography using a literary form, *The Story of Ruby Bridges* (Coles, 1995). The second is a tenth-grade classroom where the students participate in a close reading of an opinion piece written by Quindlen (2001) soon after the terrorist attack on New York City.

Like any successful journey, the quest toward comprehension is dependent on navigating the trek with a destination in mind.

▶ Questions Supporting Analysis of What the Text *Says*

Initial discussion of the text is at the literal level—making use of the who/what/when/where/why/how much/how many questions we're familiar with composing. The intent of these questions is to promote thinking about the key ideas and details the author is sharing. Grasping the gist of the text lays a foundation to help students move beyond a surface level of understanding. This initial understanding will deepen as students engage in additional analysis of other features of the text. Questions that help readers gain this general text understanding ask, *What's the problem? What's the cause? Where did this happen? Under what circumstances did this happen?* Be careful to ask for key details that are essential to developing a deeper meaning and to avoid those questions that are not essential.

Third-Grade Reading/Language Arts

The Story of Ruby Bridges (Coles, 1995) is about the bravery and strength of a child and caring adults to persevere in an angry 1960s New Orleans community that was newly desegregated. But young readers will have a difficult time understanding how brave and strong Ruby needed to be if they don't understand what was unfair about the schools, how it was a judge who ordered Ruby to attend a formerly all-white elementary school, and how Ruby's parents and Ruby herself felt about going to a new school. All of these details give the reader an understanding of the reality of New Orleans at the time but also the enormous pressure Ruby must have felt. She carried with her the feelings of the judge, her parents, and herself as she walked to school on the very first day.

Third-grade teacher Jared Silvers knew that helping his students understand the details of the text was the gateway to their intuiting the broader meaning of the text. Mr. Silvers created the following text-dependent questions to frame initial discussions with his third graders, with the intention of getting students to investigate the text for the purpose of building a foundational understanding:

- What was unfair about the schools in New Orleans?
- Who decided that Ruby would attend William Frantz Elementary School?
- How did Ruby's parents feel about her being chosen to go to an all-white school?
- What was it like for Ruby when she walked into her new school on the first day?

By understanding the key details of what schools were like in New Orleans, who ordered Ruby to go to the school, and how her parents felt about Ruby going, as well as how Ruby felt, Mr. Silvers believed his students would have the foundational knowledge needed to understand her bravery and strength. Notice how his questions pushed students to identify the key details that unlocked the general understanding that eventually, through more readings, led to their deeper understanding that *"what transpired in the fall of 1960 in New Orleans would forever change my life and help shape a nation"* (Coles, 1995, p. 1). However, key details are not trivial. Be careful when designing key detail questions to ask ones that are significant enough to support a general understanding of the text. Mr. Silvers could have asked the following text-dependent questions that would have done nothing to unlock a deeper understanding of the text:

- How old was Ruby when she left Mississippi? (four years old)
- What was the name of the school the three black girls were sent to? (McDonough 19)
- How did Ruby look, and what did she carry on her way to school every day? (clean dress, bow in her hair, a lunch pail)

Tenth-Grade English

The next example illustrates the key detail questions asked of a class of tenth graders reading the article "A Quilt of a Country" by Anna Quindlen, which appeared in *Newsweek* on September 27, 2001. The complexity of this informational text lies in its use of historical references and reflections by the writer in noting the country's strengths as a multicultural society, and its tendency to divide once again after the initial unifying shock of a national tragedy has faded. The article begins by comparing the country to a quilt:

> America is an improbable idea. A mongrel nation built
> of ever-changing disparate parts, it is held together by a
> notion, the notion that all men are created equal, though
> everyone knows that most men consider themselves
> better than someone. "Of all the nations in the world,
> the United States was built in nobody's image," the
> historian Daniel Boorstin wrote. That's because it was
> built of bits and pieces that seem discordant, like the
> crazy quilts that have been one of its great folk-art forms,
> velvet and calico and checks and brocades. Out of many,
> one. That is the ideal. (Quindlen, 2001)

Tenth-grade English teacher Oshah Lin developed text-dependent questions about the literal meaning of the text to purposefully lead students to a more critical understanding later. In so doing, she fostered the foundational knowledge her students would need to support their deeper understanding of the author's attitude about the United States in the days after 9/11:

- When was this article written, and why is that significant?
- What is the United States compared to?
- What "notion" does the writer say holds the United States together?
- What observation does the historian make about the United States?

Importantly, she didn't ask students the name of the historian, or the types of fabric used. These details don't lead anywhere in particular, and for that reason may not be necessary in a discussion of what the text says, even though answering the questions would require the students to return to the text.

The details that students were being asked to identify in these two texts were initially supportive of a general understanding aimed at locating central themes or concepts. These weren't just interesting details; they were key to developing this understanding. For *Ruby Bridges*, a literary text reliant on a narrative form, the questions were about the characters, the conflict, and the attempts to resolve the conflict. Questions for narrative forms should support students in eventually understanding the deeper meaning behind the character or plot conflicts. For the informational article "A Quilt of a Country," the questions focused on big ideas and a major detail that frames the development of a general understanding of this text.

▶ Questions Supporting Analysis of How the Text *Works*

The second phase of text-dependent questions is designed to help the reader analyze *how the text works* internally. These types of questions encourage students to inspect the author's craft or style of presenting information, the vocabulary used to share the message, and the expository or story grammar structures used to convey the message. The author's craft refers to the use of techniques such as language devices in a narrative (simile, metaphor, personification, parallel structures), to the word choices used to create the mood and tone, and to the use of techniques such as flashback and foreshadowing to support inferences about the theme. The author's craft is also reflected in the point of view, in how problems and solutions are shared, and in how arguments are made.

You will recall from previous chapters that vocabulary words and phrases impact text complexity in two important ways. First, they signal the organizing structures used by the writer. In the early years of school, students get fairly proficient at identifying a structure by focusing on signal words such as *if . . . then* to signal a cause and effect, and *first, next, then* to note chronology. But as texts become more sophisticated for older readers, the vocabulary the author chooses to contextualize the structure may not be as easy to identify. Phrases like *not long after* signal chronology, but more subtly. Second, these vocabulary words and phrases label concrete objects and actions (*electron microscope; remembered*) and abstract concepts (*socioculturally relevant; dissolve*). The temptation is to locate the multisyllabic words and teach them to students. But keep in mind that during a close reading, the students are reading multiple times. That being so, the vocabulary words and phrases that may prove vexing might also contain opportunities for students to apply problem-solving strategies to resolve unknown meanings. If, for instance, the meaning of an unknown word can be cracked using structural analysis skills (affixes, root, base), then develop questions that encourage students to do so. If an unknown phrase can be resolved using contextual analysis (i.e., definition, explanation, synonym, contrast, or punctuation), then develop questions that prompt students to seek out these clues. Text-dependent questions should help readers focus on the word choices the author used to organize the text and on the techniques that were used to tell the story or share the information or make the argument. Let's return to the two classroom examples to examine questions that focus students' attention on how the text works.

Text-dependent questions should help readers focus on the word choices the author used to organize the text, and on the techniques that were used to tell the story, share the information, or make the argument.

Third-Grade Reading/Language Arts

After Mr. Silvers assessed that his students now possessed a general understanding of the story, he reread a portion of the picture book and asked additional questions that pushed them to a deeper understanding of

Ruby's character. His intention was to strengthen their understanding of how the author used cause-and-effect structures to explain events:

- How did Ruby act when she saw the crowd of people each morning?
- How did Ruby react when she entered the classroom?
- Why did Mrs. Henry question Ruby?
- Look at the illustrations on pages 19–20. Why did Ruby stop in front of the screaming people?

Analyzing the development of the characters is a significant factor that comes into play when students are attempting to understand the structure of a text using a narrative form. As Mr. Silvers listened to the following conversation among his students, he assessed their understanding of the cause-and-effect structure used by the author to highlight the South's attempts at desegregation. He also noted the ways in which his students came to understand the role that individuals played in causing this to occur, and witnessed how that realization had, in turn, deepened their overall understanding of Ruby's character.

Jacob: Ruby was scared when she saw the crowd of people every morning.

Ethan: It doesn't say that. I think she was brave.

Jacob: It doesn't say that exactly, but it says Ruby first walked slowly but then she walked quickly. She walked faster when she saw the angry crowd of people. I do that when I have to walk past that creepy house on the corner.

Addison: Oh yeah, I agree. It's like at first she was just walking slowly like those angry people didn't bother her, but then she walked fast so she could hurry and get into the classroom. I think that really shows she's brave.

Jacob: I'm brave 'cause I walk past that scary house. But I don't know how brave I'd be with people yelling at me. She's braver 'n me.

Mr. Silvers turned the small-group discussions back to the two language charts the students were developing. One chart chronicled cause-and-effect examples, while the other listed events in chronological order. The teacher knew that by listing these events, his students would develop a keener awareness of Ruby's actions in the face of threats.

Tenth-Grade English

Ms. Lin also asked text-dependent questions designed to push her students' thinking about how the author used a compare-and-contrast structure to support her argument that the country endures despite conflicts between groups:

- What positive and negative connotative words are being used? Why?
- How does the writer help you figure out what *pluralistic* means?
- Why does the writer pose so many questions? What effect does this have on a reader?
- What contradictions does the writer point out?

Another technique Quindlen used was to cite authoritative sources to support her argument. Ms. Lin knew that a major factor contributing to the complexity of this essay was the book's intertextuality, as it made reference to other works, including *Portnoy's Complaint* (Roth, 1969/1994) and Studs Terkel's collection of essays from *Working* (1974), neither of which she expected her students to have read. Therefore, she drew her students' attention to the sentences where these texts were mentioned, and then briefly explained the significance of each.

"So these would probably be books that Anna Quindlen read, right?" asked Hector. "And that the people who were reading the magazine would know, too?"

The conversation continued, as Ms. Lin again asked what effect the number of questions the writer used had on the readers. Before long, the class settled on *uncertainty* as one connotation of the text. Elena explained:

> There was so much uncertainty after 9/11, and everyone was scared. Quindlen was scared, too. She's asking so many questions because everyone was uncertain about what would happen next. But then she cites experts, so it calms you down, like someone's in control.

The questions asked by each of these teachers helped readers figure out how the text worked; they were not just an academic exercise. In both cases, the vocabulary, author's craft, and text structure were furthering the students' critical analysis of the text, not just reinforcing its superficial meaning. When developing questions to support this type of analysis, consider the text's structural organization: was it a cause-and-effect structure, a sequence- or chronology-of-information structure, a problem-and-solution structure, a description structure, or a compare-and-contrast structure? If the text employs a narrative form, questions that address the character or plot development work well. Also consider any literary devices that were used, such as metaphor, alliteration, or analogy, and explore how effective they were at adding clarity to the meaning. Was evidence or data shared, and if so, was it effective in supporting the development of information being addressed? What words, phrases, and language did the author use to convey the meaning? As the students in the previous examples continued to analyze the two texts at hand, they were building on their general understanding of what the text said by looking at how the author made the text work. All of these layered and integrated insights were moving them toward understanding each text's deeper meaning.

▶ Questions Supporting Analysis of What the Text *Means*

Students who have a firm grasp on the literal meaning and structural elements of a text are better equipped to engage in interpretative and critical analyses of the text's meaning. The text-dependent questions designed for this phase of instruction cause the readers to return to each text once again to evaluate its aesthetic or content quality, its influence on the reader, and perhaps its relationship to other texts on the same topic. To be sure, the questions themselves are more complex, as they are not readily answered with a simple reply. Instead, these questions often spark debate as students wrestle with the meaning. As well, they are listening to the views of others, some of whom may have thoughts and opinions that are not in agreement with their own. In this phase, the teacher's skills as a facilitator of discourse are on full display.

Third-Grade Reading/Language Arts

By now, Mr. Silvers's students were asking to see and listen to certain passages and illustrations as he posed questions.

"What part did Mrs. Henry play to integrate schools?" he asked, and Shannon asked for him to read the part where Ruby's teacher sat with her all day in the principal's office the first day of school, when neither of them could enter the classroom due to the chaos outside.

"The teacher made sure Ruby didn't get too afraid. That helped her be brave," said David.

Mr. Silvers asked his students to determine the author's attitude toward his subject, always asking them to provide evidence to support their ideas. The longest discussion happened when he asked them to compare Ruby's experiences with those of other U.S. civil rights leaders they had been studying, especially Dr. Martin Luther King Jr. and Rosa Parks.

"How are her actions similar to or different from those of these two?" he asked. Several students said that they were different because Ruby was a child, while the others were adults who chose to be leaders.

"I think that because Ruby was a little girl, it reminded lots of parents about their own kids," offered Lacey. "It would make them think harder about segregation," she added. The timeline the class had developed for *Ruby Bridges* helped them to put the event into a context.

"Rosa Parks came first, so that was really brave," said Kendra.

"And Dr. King, he started in 1957, so it's . . . it's three years before Ruby had to go to school," said Lacey. "But that's not long. That's like when we were in kindergarten."

With Mr. Silvers's help, they saw how the events in New Orleans could be added to the civil rights timeline they were developing.

"She's important, 'cause that was the first time a child was involved," said Rodrigo. Notice how these questions pushed the readers to think more deeply about how the people in the story were part of the civil rights movement. If students had not developed their understanding of the characters, their motives, and their actions, they would not have been able to see the effects this important time in history had on key players.

Tenth-Grade English

Ms. Lin asked her students the following text-dependent questions to spur discussion about the essay's inferential meaning:

- What is the author's attitude toward our nation?
- Why did Quindlen write this?

She then posed questions that required the students to take a more critical stance, especially in looking across multiple texts. She wanted them to discuss the message of the text and how it might be similar or different if written in 2015, rather than in 2001. The teacher, referring to an essay they had discussed earlier called "The Condition of Black Life Is One of Mourning" (Rankine, 2015), asked, "How does Quindlen's message square with Rankine's?" Her students pulled their annotated copies of this second essay from their folders.

"The sentence I keep coming back to [in Rankine's essay] is 'When blacks become overwhelmed by our culture's disorder and protest (ultimately to our own detriment, because protest gives the police justification to militarize, as they did in Ferguson), the wrongheaded question that is asked is, What kind of savages are we? Rather than, What kind of country do we live in?'" Justine said. This, in turn, sparked debate about the symbolism of a quilt and the use of fabric as a metaphor.

"The thing is, it can tear. Like, it's only as strong as the weakest stitches," offered Ana.

"How can we stay strong as a country if we turn on each other?" asked Ms. Lin, challenging their thinking even further. "Is Quindlen's piece reflective of U.S. society today?"

If questions like these had not been asked, many students might have concluded that the purpose of the text was simply to show how both positive and negative words could be used to describe the United States. However, Ms. Lin's questions caused them to think about the country more deeply. She pushed them to think about the author and to consider her perspective, which, in turn, led them to come to a deeper understanding regarding bias and the effects it can have on readers. By drawing on students' previous work with another piece, she also pressed them to critically analyze both texts.

▶ Conclusion

Teachers can involve students in close reading experiences as a way to engage in deep text analysis. As students become skilled with this approach, they will be able to access increasingly complex text both with their peers and independently. As we argued earlier in this book, teaching students to read and understand complex texts begins with an understanding of what makes a text complex. Teachers, not computers, need to analyze texts and determine the instructional match between the texts and their students. Thankfully, a number of resources are available for teachers, including quantitative readability formulas and qualitative assessment tools that can be used in these analyses. In addition, teachers need to consider the readers themselves, as well as the task students will be expected to complete with the text, before making a final selection.

Having said that, we must commit to our students and help them read increasingly complex texts, and read those texts well. The examples we have shared are intended to provide you with the means to free yourselves to craft the close reading experiences that support your particular students in accomplishing the purpose of each lesson. While limited frontloading of information by the teacher should occur during close reading, these examples demonstrate that, while the close reading path takes many directions, they all are designed to ensure that students gain competency in knowing how to independently analyze a text. There is no "set in stone" way that this must happen. Revisit the examples that we've shared, and you'll realize that every decision the teachers made about the features that needed to be analyzed, the questions that needed to be asked, and the number of times the text needed to be reread was dependent on the developing competencies of their students as readers who could deeply analyze a text.

Exploring Teacher-Led Tasks

Scaffolded Reading Instruction of Complex Texts

Reading instruction is being shaped by the call to use increasingly complex texts in classrooms, beginning with the youngest readers. We support this call, as these texts can be useful for fostering comprehension, with guidance and support from the teacher. In the previous two chapters, we discussed the teacher-led tasks of modeling and close reading as essential methods for teaching with complex texts. In this chapter, we argue that a third teacher-led task—scaffolded reading—is important for building the capacity of readers to engage with increasingly complex texts. We hold this as an approach distinct from guided reading with leveled texts (e.g., Fountas & Pinnell, 1999). On the surface, these approaches appear similar, because both scaffolded and guided reading practices involve students in small, homogenous groups working with the teacher. However, they are fundamentally different because of the teaching intentions and the text being used.

▶ Teaching Intentions

The Report of the National Reading Panel asserts that there are five critical components, or pillars, of reading instruction in Grades K–8: phonemic awareness, phonics, fluency, vocabulary, and comprehension (National Institute of Child Health and Human Development, 2000). These are widely recognized as critical in the reading process, and a student who has difficulty with one or more of these components will struggle to read at expected levels. More recently, Cervetti and Hiebert (2015) identified a sixth pillar— knowledge development—as an equally essential component of a reading instruction program. The authors cite evidence that when the reader possesses a higher level of background knowledge about the content he or she is reading, there is a positive effect on comprehension, accuracy, and fluency. While widely recognized as being crucial to the reading and understanding of informational texts, background knowledge informs readers of literary texts as well (Pennell, 2014).

In guided reading, the scaffolds come from the text itself, with the teacher taking a backseat. In scaffolded reading, it is the teacher who is the primary source of the scaffolds.

Teaching intentions fall into six broad categories, which can be further grouped into two types: those that deal with constrained skills and those that deal with unconstrained skills (Paris, 2005). Constrained reading skills are those that have well-defined boundaries that limit their scope and set size such that they can be easily tracked and counted. Constrained reading skills include alphabetics (twenty-six letters in English), phonemes (forty-four sounds in English), phonics (the ability to connect the sounds of the language with letter combinations), and oral and silent reading fluency (both rate and accuracy). Some of these are more highly constrained than others, but the point is that once students have mastered these, they're done. Even measures of fluency, which develop over a longer period of time for readers making expected progress, top out at eighth grade (Hasbrouck & Tindal, 2006). Importantly, alphabetics, phonemic awareness, and phonics are associated with early reading development, with attention being given to automaticity. Without question, these are vital skills for developing readers to master, and are a hallmark of effective primary-grade reading programs.

But what about the unconstrained skills? These are the reading skills that have no end point, in that they continue to develop across a lifetime.

Paris (2005) notes that vocabulary and comprehension are unconstrained, as is the aspect of fluency related to prosody, or the use of emphasis, intonation, pauses, and so on. In addition, we add Cervetti and Hiebert's (2015) sixth pillar of knowledge development as an unconstrained skill. Consider your own prosody, vocabulary, comprehension, and knowledge. You are likely stronger in these areas now than you were five years ago. Better yet, you'll be even better in these areas five years into the future. However, a challenge is that vocabulary, comprehension, and knowledge are not as easy to measure as constrained skills, which rely on a counting function. Assessment of unconstrained skills takes more time, requires a higher level of assessor skills, and utilizes more sophisticated measurement systems.

It's vital for teachers to understand learning intentions in order to make teaching decisions. If the learning intentions involve alphabetics, phonemic awareness, phonics, automaticity, and fluency—the constrained skills—then guided reading instruction with carefully leveled texts makes a great deal of sense. Accordingly, guided reading with leveled text is quite useful in K–2 classrooms, as students are actively developing these skills. The leveled readers associated with guided reading are designed to provide emergent and early readers with short texts comprising controlled vocabulary and other word-level features that are matched to a reader's current skills. Guided reading lessons are typically between fifteen and thirty minutes in length, depending on the needs and stamina of the students. Stamina is a legitimate consideration for guided reading because this intensive instructional time may be the most cognitively demanding period of the day for students. Because the group is small and instructionally similar, the pacing of these lessons is quicker than those occurring at other times of the day. During guided reading, the teacher's purpose is twofold: to observe how students are consolidating syntax, graphemes, and semantic cues to read unfamiliar text, and to make decisions about the type of text being read to promote accurate and independent word recognition. For this reason, the vocabulary and knowledge demands of the text are reduced to meet the reader where he or she currently is decoding.

But the intellectual skills of young readers outstrip their decoding skills. In other words, students can listen, think, reason, and consider at far higher levels than these specialized reading materials can offer. As well, guided reading with leveled texts doesn't fully capture the learning intentions of reading teachers, who are also teaching students the unconstrained skills of prosody, vocabulary, comprehension, and knowledge development that are so intrinsic to reading. In short, there should be times when students are working with texts that stretch them a bit more.

As we have noted throughout this book, the complexity of a text is determined by considering four dimensions: the quantitative measures, the qualitative values, the reader, and the task. Scaffolded reading is a teacher-led task, and one during which students are working with at- or near-grade-level texts. However, because they are in a small, homogenous group, they are able to benefit from more frequent and intensive scaffolds delivered by the teacher. The source of the scaffolds is fundamentally different—in guided reading, the scaffolds come from the text itself, with the teacher taking a backseat. In scaffolded reading, it is the teacher who is the primary source of the scaffolds.

When much of students' reading diet is restricted to texts they can decode independently and with a high degree of accuracy, they miss out on the content that is developmentally appropriate for them to learn.

This distinction is especially critical in the case of older readers who are reading well below grade level. Those hardest-to-teach students need the scaffolding that their teacher can supply much more than they need the scaffolds that come from the text. The unintended consequence of restricting access to texts matched with students' current reading level is that they fail to make progress in their vocabulary, comprehension, and knowledge development, placing them at risk of falling further behind with each passing year. Keep in mind that a struggling eleven-year-old reader thinks like an eleven-year-old, not a seven-year-old. Restricting much of his or her interaction with texts to those written to appeal to students several years younger deprives the reader of the cognitive enrichment he or she needs to succeed. When much of students' reading diet is restricted to texts they can decode independently and with a high degree of accuracy, they miss out on the content that is developmentally appropriate for them to learn. For this reason, we believe that the usefulness of guided reading instruction with leveled texts declines precipitously after second grade, as students making expected progress have fully consolidated constrained skills. Therefore, the time dedicated to guided reading after second grade can instead be used to far greater effect through teacher-led scaffolded reading of more challenging texts.

▶ Scaffolded Instruction of Complex Texts

Teaching students to read and understand complex literary and informational texts requires a wide range of instructional routines. As we note in other chapters of this book, teachers should read aloud to students, modeling their thinking about such things as text structure, word solving, and comprehension strategies so that skills are built and habits are formed (Regan & Berkeley, 2012). Further, students should be expected to read widely from texts that they want to read, building their background knowledge and vocabularies while developing morally, emotionally, and intellectually (Ivey & Johnston, 2013). And students should read collaboratively with their peers, discussing the information found in the texts that they read (Clark et al., 2003). These are common practices that will serve students well as new expectations for text complexity are implemented. It cannot be overstated—learners need a host of experiences with rich literary and informational texts and a sliding scale of scaffolds and supports in order to access the information contained within them.

However, teachers can unintentionally create a major gap in supporting the learning of students if a close reading of a complex text is followed not with further teacher-led scaffolded small-group instruction with similar pieces, but instead with leveled texts that are likely to be substantially less challenging. In conventional small-group reading instruction, the text is selected to match the reader, often applying the questionable decision-making model suggested by Betts (1946). As documented by Shanahan (2011), Betts (1946) simply estimated the accurate rates required for understanding, suggesting for example that students needed to be taught from texts they could read with 95 to 98 percent oral reading accuracy and with a reading comprehension of 75 to 89 percent. Others disagreed with these levels and recommended much lower rates of accuracy when instructional scaffolds are provided (e.g., Powell & Dunkeld, 1971).

Students fail to develop the habits necessary to access complex text from the very instructional arrangement that was intended to provide that access. The gradual release of responsibility framework suggests that the process is more intentional. Having implemented close reading, we have been asking ourselves where the opportunity is for students to work through a similarly challenging piece of text while benefiting from intensive teacher contact. In other words, can we level up the text during small-group scaffolded reading instruction?

Teacher-led small-group reading instruction is an important component of the learning day, as it affords teachers time to observe and interact with a small group of students for an extended period of time (usually twenty to thirty minutes). This may be the most valuable real estate in the school day, as teachers can attest to the limited opportunities to customize instruction to address the needs of an individual student. A small-group reading arrangement such as this further provides students and the teacher with the opportunity to talk at length about the learning, especially to pose questions, engage in speculation, support and challenge claims, and draw conclusions.

So doesn't it follow that this is exactly the time to ramp up the complexity level of the text? Keep in mind that the central practice of guided instruction of any kind is to provide scaffolds as needed in the form of questions to check for understanding, prompts to trigger cognitive and metacognitive thinking, and cues to shift attention to salient information when the prompts are insufficient (Fisher & Frey, 2010). The opportunity to closely observe students in the act of reading and thinking is still there. However, we believe there is value in observing what a learner does when confronted with text that challenges his or her thinking, not just his or her ability to decode and comprehend at a superficial level. We want to watch how students construct knowledge and schema, as this is the linchpin for reading analytically.

Learners need a host of experiences with rich literary and informational texts and a sliding scale of scaffolds and supports in order to access the information contained within them.

We are not suggesting that the sky is the limit and that every student should be able to read any text given the proper teacher scaffolding. Scaffolded reading is a time to stretch students to grapple with text that is more difficult than they can access on their own. This principle of scaffolding is at the heart of Vygotskian pedagogy. Reasoned selection of text should involve consideration of the content, the process students will engage in to interact with the content, and the product that will result (Tomlinson & Imbeau, 2010). These principles of differentiated instruction provide a decision-making framework for adjusting each in order to stretch, but not break, learners. They also make it clear to us that the text alone doesn't need to be the only instrument of differentiation. Fourth-grade students learning about electricity aren't expected to read *Electrical Principles and Theoretical Constructs* (we made that title up). But *The Boy Who Harnessed the Wind* (Kamkwanba & Mealer, 2012) can offer them a suitably challenging read that extends their vocabulary, critical thinking skills, and scientific understanding. By attending to the type and number of scaffolds needed (process), an observant teacher can make decisions about products, instead of simply discarding the text in favor of an easier one (content). There are at least three ways to use a scaffolded reading instruction approach with complex texts: as an extension of a close reading, as a preview for later reading, or as an opportunity to address the skill needs of specific students.

Extension of a Close Reading

Sometimes scaffolded small-group reading instruction is used as an extension of the close reading students have done. For example, following a close reading of the Silly Putty chapter from the book *Toys! Amazing Stories Behind Some Great Inventions* (Wulffson, 2000), fourth-grade teacher Marla Henderson met with small groups of students and guided their development of text-dependent questions. Her class had already learned a great deal about questioning, including the relationship between questions and answers (QAR) (Raphael & Au, 2005), and her scaffolded reading instruction focused on students reading at or above grade level so that they could develop questions they could use in their collaborative discussions with their peers. For example, Devon said that they should ask about the text structure: "The structure is chronological, and that's important because each step was important for the invention. We should ask a question about that so that we reread the text looking for all of the events that created Silly Putty." Alea added, "And we should ask about the roles that different people had because each person is important in the success of Silly Putty."

Seventh-grade English teacher Kendrick Mitchell hosted Socratic seminars (see Chapter 8) in his classroom on alternating Fridays. After initially teaching his students the procedures and processes during the first two months of the school year, he systematically turned more of the planning over to students. In advance of each Socratic seminar, he met with a rotating group of students to develop the major questions that would be posed during the discussion. Their most recent readings were drawn from their study of the Harlem Renaissance of the 1920s, and how these works inspired later generations of artists and writers. Using their main text "Fire: An Explosion of Creativity" from *Harlem Stomp!* (Hill, 2004) as a springboard, Mr. Mitchell engaged students in rereading, discussing, and eventually planning the questions. With Mr. Mitchell scaffolding their discussion, the group came up with the following:

- **Opening Question About the Text.** What words and phrases in this chapter are most important to you, and why?
- **Core Questions.** What is significant about calling African American magazines *Opportunity* and *Crisis*? What message would these titles send to black and white Americans? The writer titles this chapter "Fire."

What are the explosions he is referring to? Are these explosions destructive or constructive? What is the relationship between Langston Hughes's poem "The Weary Blues" (1926/2015) and the "explosion of creativity" the author refers to?

- **Closing Question.** Is there a "Harlem Renaissance" happening today?

"I've found that turning the question development back to students gets them to go back to the text to examine it more critically," said Mr. Mitchell. "My scaffolding comes in the form of wordsmithing their questions. I have them look more carefully at word choice to hone those questions razor-sharp. That gets them going back into the text—they show a lot more interest in the author's craft."

Preview of a Later Reading

At other times, scaffolded small-group reading instruction is used to prepare students for close reading or collaborative reading tasks. In his fifth-grade class, Bart Hopple met with small groups of students, scaffolding their reading with a text that served to build students' knowledge for the reciprocal learning they would do with primary source documents. With a group of students who were performing below grade level, Mr. Hopple used a complex text (810L), *A History of US: The First Americans* (Hakim, 2005), to guide their thinking. As they read and discussed the chapter "Plains Indians Are Not Plain at All" (pp. 42–46), Mr. Hopple asked students to describe and discuss the living conditions of the Plains Indians, their traditions and beliefs, and the changes they experienced over time.

"They used to be poor, but when they traded buffalo skins for guns, they could get more food and live better," said one student.

"Yeah, and then they didn't farm so much because they could live on the buffalo," said another. "Their way of life changed a lot."

Similarly, Jessica Anaya used teacher-led scaffolded reading with peer-led collaborative tasks. It was spring, and her second graders were just beginning to meet in short-literature circles. They were using simple chapter books to learn about literature circles. However, they needed lots of support in learning how to discuss a text so that others in the group could understand. She met with a small group who were reading *26 Fairmount Avenue* (1999), a recounting of author Tomie dePaola's early childhood as his family built a house. In one chapter, the author tells his readers about going to kindergarten.

Ms. Anaya:	We've talked before about how we think Tomie is pretty funny, even though other people don't always appreciate it. Can you find an example of that in this chapter?
Marlon:	Ooh, I know! It was . . .
Ms. Anaya:	Wait, Marlon. Be sure everyone has a chance to look first. Do you have your page ready?
Marlon:	Yeah, I forgot. [Slowly turning pages of the book.] It's in here somewhere. Yep, here it is!
Ms. Anaya:	Excellent. Put your finger on that example. [To the other students] Get your fingers ready, too, so we can talk about it. [The other students join in.] Okay, Marlon, give us your example.
Marlon:	When he left kindergarten and walked straight home!
Ms. Anaya:	Tell us more about that. Help us get on the right page so we can read it with you.
Marlon:	Start on page 34 where it says, "I went up to a lady who looked like she might be the teacher."
Ms. Anaya:	Where should we stop?
Marlon:	On the next page. The last sentence is, "I walked right out of the school and all the way home."
Ms. Anaya:	[To the other students] Now, before we talk about it, reread that section to yourself, then Marlon can explain his thinking.

Ms. Anaya's students learned how to use examples from the text, and let their classmates know in advance what passage they would be speaking about. By slowing down the conversation just a bit, Ms. Anaya created a space for students to reread in advance of discussion. "One of the things I've noticed is that they seem to be getting better at listening to each other," she said. "The rereading gets them paying attention to someone else's ideas, instead of only thinking about what they are going to say next."

There are times when it is wise to preview a text with a small group before a close reading occurs in order to increase students' understanding. Education specialist Jenna Robertson met in advance with a small group of students, several with identified disabilities, in their tenth-grade English class while the rest of the class engaged in collaborative learning or scaffolded reading with their English teacher. Ms. Robertson and general education teacher Arturo Macias cotaught the course, and regularly used scaffolded reading instruction to preview challenging texts with students who needed it "warmed up," as Ms. Robertson says. During a unit anchored by the novel *Life of Pi* (Martel, 2001), Ms. Robertson met periodically with the group to preview sections Mr. Macias would be using with the entire class in close reading lessons. The English teacher selected a critical passage near the end of the book, and the special educator knew several students who would benefit from preteaching in advance of Mr. Macias's lesson.

In qualitatively analyzing the text, Ms. Robertson determined that this selection marked a departure from the rest of the text because the narration shifted from first person to third. In addition, this section was challenging because the events were reported differently to two disbelieving government authorities, casting doubt in the reader's mind about whether the entire story was not as it seemed. To prepare them for Mr. Macias's close reading, Ms. Robertson previewed the passage with six students and helped them make connections to other unreliable narrators they had encountered previously, as one student noted, "like the guy in 'The Tell-Tale Heart'" (Poe, 1843/2002).

After rereading Pi's second account of the story, the teacher turned the students' attention to the passage where one of the officials listed the similarities between the first story, which featured animals, and the second, in which all of the calamities befell humans. "Let's make our own list of the similarities between the two so you can refer back to them later," said the teacher. "Mr. Macias's lesson is going to focus on which story we choose to believe, and you'll have to decide if the author gives you enough evidence to persuade you one way or the other."

Addressing Specific Student Needs

Scaffolded small-group reading instruction can also be used to address the assessed needs of specific students. For example, sixth-grade science teacher Jorge Cabrera noticed that several students were still having difficulty with comparing and contrasting. He met with them to provide scaffolded reading instruction while the rest of the class engaged in collaborative or independent learning tasks. In this case, he used a selection from a science textbook, specifically a section about three major rock types. He asked the students to read the first section, focused on igneous rocks.

When they finished the couple of paragraphs, he asked them to discuss the text and summarize their discussion on a compare-and-contrast graphic organizer. He noted that his students were able to do this successfully. The students were then asked to read the section on sedimentary rocks, which they did. Then Mr. Cabrera asked them to update their graphic organizers before talking with their peers. They had difficulty with the similarities, but successfully identified a number of differences. He focused their conversation on the ways that these two types of rocks were similar. "Remember," he noted, "we have to both compare and contrast, meaning that we have to think about how two things are similar and how they are different. Let's focus for now on the similarities. Let's look back at the text and see what we can find." This process continued, as students read a complex piece of text, with the support of their teacher, practicing the skill that they needed to develop.

Claudia Alexander was seated at a table with five first graders who were struggling with comprehension. For that reason, she called this small group together—to deliver teacher-directed scaffolded reading instruction. She selected the poem "Chang McTang McQuarter Cat" by John Ciardi (1987) as a means for teaching comprehension strategies related to character development. Ciardi uses a poetic form to describe the contradictions in a cat, which begins:

> Chang McTang McQuarter Cat
> Is one part this and one part that.
> One part is yowl, one part is purr.
> One part is scratch, one part is fur.
> One part, maybe even two
> Is how he sits and stares right through
> You and you and you and you.
> And when you feel my Chang-Cat stare
> You wonder if you're really there. (p. 36)

Ms. Alexander began by charting responses from students regarding the characteristics of cats, emphasizing the actions associated with feline behavior. Next she distributed copies of the poem and invited her students to read a poem about a cat named Chang McTang and to look for characteristics the poet spotlights. As they read quietly, she moved around the table to listen to the reading of individual students, taking anecdotal notes as she went. After they read it through twice, she turned their attention back to the chart they had constructed. "Let's compare the characteristics of cats we listed, and match them to places where the poet wrote similar ideas," she said. For the next ten minutes, she and the students annotated the language chart and the copies of the poem, creating a list of phrases the poet used to describe cat behaviors. Ms. Alexander later said, "My students' decoding skills are pretty good, but they do not understand much of what they're reading. I've been working with this group for the last few weeks to strengthen their ability to anticipate what a writer will say about something, and then to look for that information."

▶ **Conclusion**

Our review of the research, not to mention our direct experiences, suggests that instruction with leveled texts has not paid the dividends promised. As students are learning to read, practicing with highly decodable books filled with high-frequency words, sight words, and patterns is important so that students develop automaticity (Snow, Burns, & Griffin, 1998). But the practice of routinely using leveled texts with older students has been problematic, and far too many students are in leveled texts all the way though school, until they drop out. We can change that. But we're not suggesting that everything change. Evidence-based reading instruction continues to require expert teacher modeling, small-group instruction, formative assessments, and attention to all aspects of literacy (e.g., phonemic awareness, phonics, fluency, vocabulary, and comprehension). It's just that small-group scaffolded reading instruction should not *rely* on the text as a primary scaffold. All students should have access to complex texts and the opportunity to learn with texts beyond those that we have incorrectly considered to be at their instructional level. It's time to ramp up the text complexity levels as part of the scaffolded instruction that teachers provide. We hope that will allow for increased expectations for students such that they think critically about the information contained in the texts they read. When that is done, students will no longer be sentenced to reading texts that are far below their grade level, essentially independently, in the presence of their teacher. Instead, the teacher will serve as a primary scaffold, assisting students up the staircase of text complexity.

Our review of the research, not to mention our direct experiences, suggests that instruction with leveled texts has not paid the dividends promised.

In the past, our profession may have been a bit complacent, waiting for students to develop in their literacy skills. That time is over. If we can put a person on the Moon, we can ensure that students are able to read about it. If we can create the Internet, we have the responsibility to ensure that all students can access and evaluate the information contained therein. And if we expect to solve the problems present in the world today, problems our ancestors could not have imagined, then we must ensure that students can think deeply, look for evidence, and justify their ideas and proclamations.

Exploring Peer-Led Tasks

Collaborative Conversations and Peer-Mediated Learning

Readers benefit from discussions with peers about challenging texts. In the company of peers, students can ask each other questions, entertain ideas, and draw conclusions. Most of all, peer-led tasks can promote new understandings of material that some students might not realize they didn't comprehend. In other words, collaborative conversations can provide access to more complex texts than a reader might fully understand on his or her own. Consider this exchange among a group of tenth graders in their biology class. The class was studying ecology and had read a section of a text focused on the flow of energy in an ecosystem.

Duane: I have a question. I read the part about the food chain representing energy transfer, but does it always have to go from producer to herbivore?

Paige: I think that it was just an example that there can be lots of steps in a food chain.

Cody: Yeah, I agree. The figure on page 43 has a food chain, going from producer to herbivore to omnivore to carnivore. I know that the carnivore, the snake on that page, isn't going to eat the plant or probably the grasshopper, so I think it works for this example.

Duane: But does it always have to be that way?

Paige: I don't think so. Like some omnivores eat plants and insects, so it could skip the grasshopper from that picture. The mouse could eat the plant or the grasshopper.

Cody: And some animals really do eat just about anything. I'm thinking of crows and pigs. They eat whatever they can get. So they would have a lot of arrows [pointing to diagram] coming to them and then some things that eat them.

Paige: I think the bears are omnivores, too. But when I went to the zoo, they said that some bears are pretty much only carnivores and others are pretty much only herbivores. The guide said that it really depends on what food sources are available in their habitat.

This brief exchange demonstrates how these biology students spent time understanding and questioning a central idea in their reading. Although the diagram seemed clear, the students needed to speculate, discard ideas, and raise new—and as of yet unanswered—questions in order to make sense of this science concept. But without the opportunity to do so, students like Duane might have been left with unanswered questions. In a large group, Duane might have been reluctant to pose such a question. But within a small group, he had a secure forum to do so. The task that the teacher created was intentional, too. She didn't just say, "Turn to your partner and talk about the diagram on page 43." Instead, she gave the students a task to complete, asking them to produce a one-minute screencast explaining how energy flows through an ecosystem. The task, it seems, drove Duane to focus on the details so that the group could produce an accurate digital video explanation for their classmates. While Duane's group chased down the specifics of energy flow, other groups were charged with addressing related issues about bioaccumulation and net primary productivity.

▶ Conditions That Support Peer-Led Tasks

The discussion in the biology class was driven by a task, in this case, to produce a screencast to teach others about a scientific concept. Peer-led tasks offer an excellent way for students to uncover the details of a text for authentic reasons. But these students weren't just automatically able to work together productively. Their teacher created the conditions that allowed for meaningful collaboration to occur. In point of fact, she carefully selected the text, created a meaningful task, and taught her students how to resolve problems collectively.

Text Selection

When students are invited to collaborate, the texts can be complex but perhaps not as complex as those used by teachers when modeling and providing close reading instruction. Nevertheless, the texts used during group work should also not be so easy as to remove any challenge or struggle from the experience because we want students to have opportunities to independently use the skills they are learning about how to wrestle with a text. As we discussed in Chapter 1, struggle is important to learning, and this is especially true in group work when students have peer support and interaction to guide their understanding. Quite frankly, a text that doesn't have some challenge to it isn't likely to spark much debate and discussion. But when ideas are thought-provoking, students have authentic reasons to interact with one another. "What do you think?" they ask. "Why do you think so? I don't agree, so help me understand," they say as they push one another to think more deeply.

Authentic Tasks

It is unlikely, however, that these discussions will occur in the absence of an equally thought-provoking task. What students are asked to *do* with the text is as important as the text itself. In fact, publishers of adult literary and informational texts have known this for many years, and for this reason include discussion guides for book clubs to use. How often have you peeked at the questions posed as you read? And more important, how often did the questions themselves give you a new insight into what you were reading? In other words, the best tasks are those that assist a group of readers in elevating their thinking from the level of basic comprehension to that of critical analysis and debate.

Productive Failure

Students don't automatically know how to collaborate. They may have collaborated in the past, but not with the current content and perhaps not with their current peer group. They need to be taught how to collaborate and what each of their teachers expects in terms of group work. It's not fair to ask students to collaborate in class if they have not been taught how to do this.

Students don't automatically know how to collaborate. They need to be taught how to collaborate and what each of their teachers expects in terms of group work.

As part of learning how to collaborate, students need to be taught to discuss topics in ways that keep the group moving forward. This is especially true because we expect groups to meet with productive failure (Kapur, 2008). This is a state of learning we actively strive for, and is based on the reminder that one learns from one's mistakes. When a task is too easy, groups typically divide the work and go their separate ways until they meet again to assemble the pieces. Ideally, the task should be difficult enough so that students have a reason to talk with one another to resolve their confusions. Resolving errors is a major element of group discussions, and peer-led tasks should provide students time to work together to clarify their understanding of skills and concepts they are learning. In order to do so, they must first have a task that is sufficiently complex such that errors can occur. We've said a lot about errors before—making mistakes is an essential part of the learning process. However, as students make mistakes, there are likely to be moments of argument and debate. As we remind them, "It's okay to disagree. It's not okay to be disagreeable."

▶ Accountable Talk to Support Peer-Led Tasks

Accountable talk, described by Michaels, O'Connor, and Resnick (2008) as the academic discourse of learners as they discuss, clarify, question, provide evidence, disagree, and develop solutions, forms the heart of classroom discourse. It moves students from conversation to true discussion. Accountable talk has three main components. Everyone is accountable to (1) the classroom community, (2) the knowledge base, and (3) reasoned logic. The entry point for young students involves being able to listen to one another (K–2), report on the ideas of others (Grades 3–5), and extend the ideas of others with their own (Grades 6–12). These accountable talk practices are featured in teacher-led discussions, with the intention that students will then transfer these skills to peer-led tasks.

Learning the procedures of accountable talk involves giving students discussion prompts that allow them to carry on a conversation with a partner or to encourage one another to elaborate on an idea about a text. At first, these text-based discussions are a bit on the simpler side, and the texts the learners talk about are a little less complex than they would otherwise be. This is done to create the cognitive space students need when learning a new procedure. As students learn how to work in a group, the selected text becomes more challenging. Accountable talk can be further scaffolded using language frames. For instance, the following frames provide students with examples they can use when talking with their group members:

- I agree that _____.
- A point that needs emphasizing since so many people believe the opposite is that _____.
- While I don't agree that _____, I do recognize that _____.
- The evidence shows that _____.
- My own view, however, is that _____.

However, it is important to state that, as scaffolds, language frames can be overused and misused. The key to their use lies in understanding what scaffolds really are: temporary frames used to support discourse that is under construction. As such, they should be faded as the year progresses. Over time, students should be internalizing these frames as ways to hold discussions with one another. We've also been in lots of classrooms where language frames are displayed with little thought given as to how and why they are used. Instead, they should be categorized by their functions. As an example, written language frames should perform specific tasks (see Figure 8.1).

These frames should be introduced throughout the year as others are faded, and they should ideally be displayed on table tents so that they are immediately accessible. As with all learning, the integration of language frames such as these should progress such that the language students are using becomes increasingly more sophisticated and nuanced.

Figure 8.1   Argumentation Language Frames

Making a Claim	I observed _____ when _____.
	I compared _____ and _____.
	I noticed _____ when _____.
	The effect of _____ on _____ is _____.
Providing Evidence	The evidence I use to support _____ is _____.
	I believe _____ [statement] because _____ [justification].
	I know that _____ is _____ because _____.
	Based on _____, I think _____.
	Based on _____, my hypothesis is _____.
Asking for Evidence	I have a question about _____.
	Does _____ have more _____?
	What causes _____ to _____?
	Can you show me where you found the information about _____?
Offering a Counterclaim	I disagree _____ because _____.
	The reason I believe _____ is _____.
	The facts that support my idea are _____.
	In my opinion, _____.
	One difference between my idea and yours is _____.
Inviting Speculation	I wonder what would happen if _____.
	I have a question about _____.
	I wonder why _____.
	What caused _____?
	How would this be different if _____?
	What do you think will happen if _____ / next?
Reaching Consensus	I agree _____ because _____.
	How would this be different if _____?
	We all have the same idea about _____.

Source: Adapted from Ross, Fisher, & Frey (2009). Used with permission.

Keep in mind that these language frames can sound stilted coming from the mouths of students. The goal is not to make the students sound robotic, but rather to help them build the skills they need to agree and disagree with one another, and to arrive at consensus. In order to foster more natural language, it is useful to expand these frames after they are initially learned. For example, the teacher can lead the class to develop a list of other ways to ensure that the words are the students' own. Fifth-grade teacher Ofelia Reyes asked her students to come up with other ways to ask each other to elaborate on ideas, and soon they had written a list that included, "Can you put the author's ideas into your own words?" and "Tell more about that." Ms. Reyes revisited language frames throughout the year, and faded some structures as she introduced new ones. "I remind my students that these frames are good for discussion, and they're even better for writing," she said. "I encourage them to apply similar structures in their written work to increase their academic language output."

As scaffolds, language frames can be overused and misused. The key to their use lies in understanding what scaffolds really are.

Discussions should allow students to engage in purposeful talk, using frames as needed, to manage their use of academic and domain-specific language. Further, these peer-led tasks should provide them with an opportunity to learn about themselves, each other, and the world. For example, Tom Raines, a middle school social studies teacher, regularly uses the published debates featured in *USA Today* to foster text-based discussion that is led by peers. In one lesson, students read one of two editorials on school discipline: the newspaper's position that zero-tolerance policies should be eased, or the opposing view of an education leader who argued that schools need to err on the side of safety. The teacher provided students with the following extended language frame to support their conversations:

> According to this article, a zero-tolerance policy is
> [necessary/unnecessary] because _____. First, the
> author states that _____. In addition, the author argues
> that _____. I agree with the author's claim that _____.
> However, I disagree with the claim that _____. In *my*
> opinion, _____. What's *your* opinion?

After posting the language frame on the board and discussing its purpose (to accurately summarize an article before adding one's own opinion), Mr. Raines distributed the articles and invited students to read and highlight or underline notable sections. Students then met with three other classmates who had read the same editorial to discuss the claims and evidence forwarded by the author. After annotating the article, they met with another student who had read the opposing-view editorial. At this point, students drew on the language frames supplied by the teacher to guide their discussions. First one partner, and then the other, shared the major points made by the writer, and then they both weighed in with their opinions. Once these partner conversations had taken place, the teacher invited the students back as a whole class and led a debate on the pros and cons advanced by the authors. After a lively discussion on the merits of each argument, students once again used a language frame for writing. This time, students wrote about their own opinion, using key arguments to support their position. In addition, a new language frame required them to acknowledge counterclaims:

> In my opinion, a zero-tolerance policy is [necessary/
> unnecessary] because _____. First, the author states
> that _____. In addition, some argue that _____. I agree
> with the author's claim that _____. It is important to
> acknowledge that some will argue that _____. While
> this argument has some merit, it is not as strong because
> _____. In summary, I believe a zero-tolerance policy is
> [necessary/unnecessary] because _____.

Mr. Raines understood that the series of small-group discussions he constructed would cause students to reread and examine the information in detail as well as more globally. In addition, he positioned reading and discussion as necessary prerequisites to more formal composition. "It's hard for my students to persuade, or for that matter to be persuaded, when they haven't had a chance to do that themselves. I want them applying their knowledge of the content to understand editorial commentary more deeply," he said.

▶ Routines to Support Peer-Led Tasks

There are any number of collaborative instructional routines that involve reading: reciprocal teaching, the facilitation of book clubs and literature circles, and the use of online book reviews and jigsaws, just to name a few. The caution is that if these are scheduled as *activities*, rather than as purposeful and meaningful *tasks*, students are more likely to overlook the details needed for deeper understanding. These routines are best used when there are associated purposes for students to engage with their peers. We'll spotlight several practices designed for students who sit along a continuum in terms of their levels of knowledge acquisition and understanding. Each of these practices should be considered when selecting the option that best parallels the level of critical thinking students are ready to engage in. Technology should also be considered, as it offers teachers new ways of engaging students in speaking and listening tasks. Some of the tasks described may involve the extensive use of digital technologies, but all have the aim of enhancing students' speaking and listening skills, as well as their understanding of complex texts through peer-led tasks.

There are any number of collaborative instructional routines that involve reading. The caution is that if these are scheduled as activities, rather than as purposeful and meaningful tasks, students are more likely to overlook the details needed for deeper understanding.

Knowledge Acquisition With Reader's Theater

The content of complex texts can be daunting for students working collaboratively, who may feel that the information is rushing past them too quickly. Reader's theater can create a space for students to linger for a longer period of time to absorb the content. As well, it offers a performance opportunity, which is an excellent motivator for students, and anchors the task in authentic purpose. The real learning occurs as group members plan their performance, returning again and again to the text. All of this practice contributes to fluency, prosody, and comprehension of the text. Students also gain practice reading and rereading a script, either one that was prepared for them or one they developed collaboratively, based on a literary or informational text they have studied. Students are expected to present that text to the rest of the class while others are listening. No props or costumes are required; rather, reader's theater is more like a radio show.

For example, during their investigation of Earth and the solar system, the fifth-grade students in Niecy Harris's class worked in small groups to collaboratively read and then write a reader's theater script to perform for the rest of the class, using passages from *Space Encyclopedia: A Tour of Our Solar System* (Aguilar, 2013). Groups were assigned entries based on constellations, the Milky Way, types of stars, and the planets in our solar system. The students constructed a script using the author's words, then rehearsed their scripts over several days. With reader's theater, there is no expectation that students memorize the script; rather, they perform a dramatic reading using the script. In this case, Ms. Harris encouraged them to project photographs from the text behind them while they performed. To ensure that the other students were benefiting from the content, Ms. Harris had her students take notes and write down questions to pose to the performers.

Knowledge Acquisition With Reciprocal Teaching

This routine is considered to provide teachers with one of the most useful and effective means for supporting students' reading comprehension, as reported by the What Works Clearinghouse (for the full report, see Institute of Education Sciences [2010]). Students read chunks of a given text and then take turns with various comprehension strategies such as predicting, questioning, clarifying, and summarizing (Palincsar & Brown, 1986). To ensure that students actually listen to one another, teachers create note-taking tools that require them to maintain a written record of the conversation. For example, the students in Angie Farlow's eighth-grade social studies class were reading the section on Abraham Lincoln from *50 American Heroes Every Kid Should Meet* (Denenberg & Roscoe, 2001). As they had been taught, they stopped at each heading to engage in their conversation, taking notes as one member *summarized*, another *clarified*, and another *questioned*, and then the last person *predicted* what might come next in the text.

Knowledge Extension With Listening Gallery Walk

Students often engage in field studies that combine community experiences with visual and narrative texts. Listening gallery walks allow students to create a visual image, record themselves talking about the image using texts they have composed, and then code the recording with a symbol that will allow others to access the digital file. One way to do this is with QR (quick response) codes that can be printed and included in the image itself. Alternatively, students can use the Aurasma app. This is an augmented reality application that allows users to create and post video to enhance a viewing experience. For example, some museums use Aurasma so that their patrons may view additional content whenever they point a smartphone or tablet at a display. In terms of classroom application, students can create their own videos and pair them with displayed work. For example, during their investigation of artists, students in Carol Bledsoe's third-grade class read widely, then visited a local art museum where they viewed the paintings of many of the artists they had read about and wanted to get to know a bit better through their paintings. When students returned, they collaborated with a partner also interested in the same artist. Together, they created narration to accompany the original artwork, which had been inspired by the works of a specific artist they viewed at the museum. When a tablet enabled with Aurasma was pointed at one of the art pieces, the video students created that accompanied the art played. When the parents visited for open house, they were able to see their children talking about their work and to learn more about the other students in the class.

Knowledge Extension With Jigsaw Presentations

After students have initially acquired information, they are ready to further expand their knowledge base through preliminary investigations. These are not culminating projects, but instead are appropriate in the middle of a unit of study. During these investigations, students work with one another on a peer-led task to research a topic and then share their findings with their peers, either in small groups or in large groups. Often, students are asked to provide their peers with feedback about their presentation skills. For example, the students in Jim Ramirez's sixth-grade science class were examining the impact of trash, including space junk, on the environment; the role of sanitation in disease prevention; and the garbage patch in the Pacific Ocean. As part of their investigation, they read *Plastic, Ahoy!* (Newman, 2014), and each group was asked to expand on one topic addressed in the book. One group focused on ocean currents and the creation of the Pacific garbage patch, using a Prezi presentation with Google Earth images and narration. Other groups focused their investigations on the mechanics of ocean gyres, the negative impact on phytoplankton, and specifics of scientific sea exploration.

Knowledge Extension With Digital Storytelling

Texts often inspire further investigation, and with younger students, these investigative experiences are typically completed collaboratively, with extensive teacher guidance. Digital storytelling is an excellent way for students to bridge what they have learned from a text and what they have investigated into the creation of their own original narrative and informational pieces. The Storybird app, for instance, provides students with access to thousands of images and photographs that can be used to illustrate original pieces of writing. These narratives are best when completed collaboratively, as this gives students plenty of opportunities to engage in meaningful discussion with one another.

The VoiceThread website (https://voicethread.com) is another digital platform that enables writers and readers to have two-way conversations. Like Storybird, students create a digital piece using the VoiceThread tools and their own illustrations and photos. In addition, they dictate the text for each page. Subsequent listeners can either listen to the writer's own voice or read the dictated script. Importantly, readers can then pose questions and offer connections that are in turn viewed by other readers. As part of their social studies curriculum, Davinia Thompson's second-grade students used VoiceThread to develop a digital book for the class that was focused on people who made a difference in their community. Her students worked in small groups to investigate local figures, including the police chief, a fire captain, and the school nurse. Ms. Thompson then compiled each group's contributions and uploaded them to the VoiceThread website. Later in their small groups, students viewed the class book and recorded their comments and questions. Ms. Thompson then had the entire class view the completed digital story, with their questions included, so they could continue the conversation about the topic.

Textual Analysis With Book Clubs or Literature Circles

As students progress through the upper elementary grades and beyond, they increasingly read and discuss texts collaboratively, often in groups of three to five students. Rather than charge groups with debriefing an entire chapter, which runs the risk of limiting students to a literal-level recounting of the text, teachers give these small groups a guiding question to consider.

As an example, consider the following discussion tenth-grade students had about Elie Wiesel's *Night* (1960), a book that explores the author's experiences with his father in the Nazi German concentration camps. The students were talking about the reasons that the Jewish people in this book did not fight back right away and, rather, went along with the plans for relocation—a guiding question provided by their teacher and meant to provoke discussion:

Marla: I don't think they really thought it would be that bad. I mean, who would have imagined that? But did you find something in the text that really shows that? We need more evidence.

Deon: Yeah, like it says right here: "Annihilate an entire people? Wipe out a population dispersed throughout so many nations? So many millions of people! By what means? In the middle of the twentieth century?" [p. 8]. They just didn't think it was possible. I agree with you.

| Jessica: | Yeah, I agree, too. But I also think it was because life was kinda normal. Yeah, they moved and lost things. But at first their life seemed kinda normal. See right here where it says, "Little by little life returned to 'normal.' The barbed wire that encircled us like a wall did not fill us with real fear. In fact, we felt this was not a bad thing; we were entirely among ourselves" [p. 11]. |
| Deon: | Exactly, that's why they didn't fight. They couldn't imagine things would ever be like they turned out, and that their lives would never get fully back to normal—that's why they didn't fight. There's lots of evidence for this. |

Students held this discussion outside the presence of their teacher, but they drew on the skills they had cultivated in terms of being accountable to one another as a learning community. These values are further evidenced through the depth of thinking that occurs in Socratic seminars. How to initiate a Socratic seminar is presented below.

Textual Analysis With Photo Narratives

This instructional practice involves having students work in teams to collect images and then record a narrative to accompany the images. It helps students leverage what they have learned from a text to explain an event or a phenomenon. For example, the first graders in Angel Munoz's classroom planted seeds, and Mr. Munoz read aloud the text *From Seed to Plant* (Gibbons, 1993) several times as the plants grew. Each day, the students took a picture of the container in which their seed was planted, and Mr. Munoz then helped them create a time-lapse video with the images using QuickTime. The student teams also captioned their photos using the information from the book and used that as an exercise to help them create narrative recordings to explain the growth of the plants and to serve as an accompaniment to the video. The teams had to consult the text repeatedly to accurately report what was occurring at each stage of growth, providing them with the chance to explore the text in greater detail.

Critical Thinking With Socratic Seminars

After students read, analyze, and discuss portions of a text, it is time for them to address the larger questions that may be raised across one or more texts. The purpose of a Socratic seminar is for students to come together to unearth issues and problems at a more global level. Although the teacher is present as a facilitator, it is not a teacher-led discussion. Rather, students pose questions to one another, with the teacher intermittently propelling the discussion forward as necessary. The teacher may pose thought-provoking questions to the group, but only with the intention of generating student discussion. This action can be particularly difficult for those who are new to Socratic seminars, as students are accustomed to addressing the teacher directly, rather than their classmates. However, it is not the teacher who is the arbiter of the knowledge, but the students themselves. Brann (1989) notes that the ultimate purpose is about "thinking things anew rather than thinking new things" (p. 106).

Sixth-grade teacher Jessica Henderson uses Socratic seminars regularly as part of her emphasis on challenging her students to think critically about texts. In a unit of study on the heroic cycle, her class read about Greek and Roman mythology and also read informational readings about the use of this narrative pattern in literature. Her students further explored the use of this device in their collaborative reading groups, using contemporary texts such as *Holes* (Sachar, 1998), *American-Born Chinese* (Yang, 2008), and *The Breadwinner* (Ellis, 2009). Ms. Henderson scheduled this Socratic seminar near the end of the unit so that students could draw on the wide range of literary and informational texts they had read. She reviewed the guidelines:

- Don't just wait to speak. Listen carefully and build off each other's ideas.
- Talk to each other, not the teacher.
- Use evidence from your texts to support your answers.
- Paraphrase accurately.

The teacher began with the essential question, "What is a hero?" and, during the hourlong discussion, posed other questions such as "What impact did the hero or heroine have on you as a reader?" and "Do our modern definitions of a hero or heroine differ from ancient ones?" Her students drew on their own collaborative readings, as well as on the informational texts the entire class had read. Ms. Henderson tallied responses so that she could make sure that all participated, and none dominated. When a vocal student was eager to answer again, she said, "Angelica, you'll be using your fifth statement, which will be your last. Do you want to use it now, or save it for later?" When she saw that one student had been listening intently but had not yet spoken, she said, "Jamal, you've been taking all this in, and I can see from your expression that you've got some ideas to add." By encouraging Angelica to listen more and Jamal to contribute his insights, she ensured that the Socratic seminar resulted in true collaboration about ideas.

▶ Conclusion

Regardless of the specific approach a teacher takes, students simply must communicate meaningfully with one another, as this is an essential practice for providing them with access to complex texts. However, the implication is that we must *teach* the communication skills, just as we teach reading comprehension, if students are to work effectively during peer-led tasks. We have to change the climate, expectations, and accountability for student-to-student interaction in classrooms everywhere. A day should not go by in which students silently try to learn content. Instead, there should be a healthy hum of learning, with many voices engaged in discussions about the topics under investigation. There are lots of different ways students learn collaboratively—from participating in brief partner talks like Think-Pair-Share, to engaging in longer whole-class group work tasks during which the teacher moves from group to group, clarifying information and providing scaffolded instruction. But again, these peer-led tasks have limited benefit if viewed by the teacher as mere activities. Rather, educators need to carefully consider the learning intentions at hand and pair them with suitable peer-led tasks. Only then will we fully realize the literacy achievements of our students—orally, digitally, and in print.

Exploring Individual Tasks

Independent learning provides a time for students to apply the skills and strategies they have practiced during teacher- and peer-led tasks to their independent reading. This is to say not that independent learning is done silently and alone, but rather that it provides all students with an opportunity to utilize their skills and strategies in their own work. The teacher is an active presence during independent learning, often meeting with each individual learner to discuss his or her work. Moreover, the teacher needs to instruct learners regarding how they can best spend their time extending their own learning through reading.

▶ Knowing How to Read Versus Being a Reader

Our purpose as teachers is not simply to teach a set of skills, but to help children and adolescents build their identities as members of a literate community. We don't want students to view reading as something that is solely a school-mandated endeavor. We want them to appreciate reading for what it can do for their minds and spirits. There's a big difference between a student who knows how to read but chooses not to unless it's required, and one who defines himself or herself as a reader. You can see the stark contrast in these two student profiles emerge when it's time for independent reading, or sustained silent reading (SSR): The former listlessly turns pages, sighs deeply, and keeps an eye on the clock, while the latter always has a book in his or her desk, backpack, or tablet, and immediately gets lost in the content. When the time is up, this reader is surprised by the interruption and begs for a few minutes more.

Our purpose as teachers is not simply to teach a set of skills, but to help children and adolescents build their identities as members of a literate community.

Barone and Barone (2015), one a reading researcher and the other an elementary reading coach, encourage teachers to define the characteristics and behaviors of readers to their students. Every teacher's goal is to cultivate his or her students' identities. By being explicit and intentional, teachers can assist students as they purposefully orchestrate a shift in their identities from individuals who *know how* to read to individuals who *are* readers. Students who are readers (Barone & Barone, 2015)

- Read every day
- Read for fun
- Talk about books
- Finish almost every book that they pick up
- Can relate to characters
- Know the genres they like to read
- Can sit for extended periods of time to read without looking around, getting up, and distracting themselves
- Read two or more books a month

The amount of reading students engage in during the school day is not a good indicator of their ability to read increasingly complex texts. Students need to engage with reading texts out of school as well as in school. In other words, reading volume matters. This was quantified in a seminal study conducted by Anderson, Wilson, and Fielding (1988) on the correlation between the number of minutes students spent reading per day and their scores on the standardized tests of the time. Children who read sixty-five minutes a day encountered more than 4,000,000 words per year, and performed at the 98th percentile on standardized tests. Contrast those results with students who spent less than five minutes a day reading: they encountered no more than 282,000 words a year, and their test performance was at the 50th percentile. What's especially disheartening is that if these two groups of students stay right where they are in terms of their reading volume, the gap between the high-volume readers and their low-volume counterparts will compound with each passing year. In ten years, the high-volume readers will have read 40,000,000 words, their counterparts only 2,820,000. In other words, the illiterate readers will not have accomplished in a decade what the motivated readers will have done in the span of six or seven months. No amount of dynamic teaching can close that chasm.

It isn't realistic to give students sixty-five minutes of each school day to read. But students who define themselves as readers are motivated to read and will seek out opportunities to do so even when it isn't for compliance. You'll recall from Chapter 1 of this book that McRae and Guthrie (2009) described five teaching practices that foster motivation in reading:

1. Relevance
2. Choice
3. Success
4. Collaboration
5. Thematic units

These practices inform the independent tasks teachers create for their students. Most of all, when students have motivation to read during the school day, that becomes the catalyst for reading on their own outside of school. When students increase the number of words encountered each day, a *practice effect* takes place. Practice does not make perfect, but it does make permanent. The skills students are taught to help them read complex texts morph into the habits they develop to understand increasingly complex texts on their own.

▶ The Case for Making Time to Read Individually

While it isn't realistic to dedicate an hour of instructional minutes per day to independent reading, we can and should regularly provide students an opportunity to read. This is accomplished in two ways: through independent reading time and through SSR. Each has its own characteristics, which we will discuss in more detail in the next sections, but for now let's concentrate on what is accomplished through the use of these instructional practices.

We'll use the analogy of physical exercise to illustrate what we mean. Talk to any athlete about his or her training regime, and you'll hear discussion of two major principles: strength and stamina. Strength-building exercises build muscle and provide the athlete with the power to kick a soccer ball or throw a baseball. In reading instruction, these exercises are analogous to the modeling and thinking aloud we do with complex texts, as well as to the close and scaffolded reading practices we enact with students. It's heavy lifting, cognitively speaking, but these practices stretch students' ability—over time—to take on increasingly challenging texts. But those same athletes also have stamina-building routines. They run or cycle for long distances so that they can extend their ability to stay in the game for its duration. In similar fashion, we build reading stamina through peer-led and independent tasks that foster endurance. The texts are somewhat less complex than the ones used with teacher-led tasks. However, sacrificing stamina-building tasks for the sake of time doesn't make sense. Athletes who build strength and ignore stamina are not able to last long in the game. Students who participate in teacher-led tasks, with little opportunity to engage in peer-led and independent tasks, fail to build reading stamina. They have more difficulty persisting with text, and have fewer self-regulatory skills to keep themselves from getting distracted.

We'll add one other element to the mix that is necessary for athletes and for readers, and that is flexibility. Athletes work on their flexibility because it bridges strength and stamina and prevents injury. Equally important is that it allows the athlete to make quick and purposeful adjustments. The quarterback who can throw the ball far and accurately but who can also scramble to avoid a tackle is going to perform better than the one who does not have the flexibility to do so. In terms of reading independently, students' development of flexibility is honed when teachers offer choices and help them make selections that are relevant to their lives. In this chapter, we will make the case for two major practices: SSR to foster flexibility, and independent reading to foster stamina. While both involve individual activities, they can and should allow for student collaboration to occur with the teacher and with peers. As you will see, these principles of reading volume and motivation come into play with each of these practices, although to differing degrees. We will first take an in-depth look at SSR, then discuss independent reading.

▶ Sustained Silent Reading

SSR is time during the day when students have an opportunity to choose books of their liking for the purpose of reading for pleasure (McCracken, 1971). No other activities occur during SSR, and all students in the class engage in silent reading simultaneously. The teacher reads for pleasure as well, providing a model of adult reading for the students. These opportunities for reading are called by many names, including Drop Everything and Read (DEAR) and Be Excited About Reading (BEAR). However, SSR is more than just setting aside ten to twenty minutes a day and telling students to read something. Pilgreen (2000), a teacher who has designed, implemented, and studied SSR programs, describes eight factors she found to be essential:

Factor 1: Access

Students need a large range and volume of reading materials to choose from. These choices should include books representing many genres on a wide variety of topics. In addition, nontraditional texts like magazines, graphic novels, and comic books should be available, as well as interesting web pages bookmarked in advance by the teacher. In order to boost access, texts should represent a wide range of reading levels, and some recorded ones should be available for students to enjoy.

Factor 2: Appeal

Appeal is closely related to access and specifically addresses the notion of what is developmentally appropriate for students. Pilgreen (2000) defines appeal as "reading materials [that] are sufficiently interesting and provocative enough for students to want to read them" (p. 9). This is especially important for intermediate and middle school students, whose interest in reading often begins to wane during these years (Kush & Watkins, 1996). Teachers can and should select texts that are culturally diverse and representative of the larger world. We should also be reminded that the texts students read should serve as both a *mirror*, such that they can see themselves, their families, and their communities, and a *window*, such that they can meet people who are very different from them (Cullinan, 1989).

As well, the topics of some narrative and informational texts may not be desirable for use during a whole class reading; however, these topics are often precisely what students *want* to read about. Books about difficult subjects can be made available during SSR in order to engage and educate students without turning it into an academic exercise. Although some topics may be uncomfortable for teachers to discuss in their classrooms, it is important that students see themselves and realistic portrayals of their lives in the books they read (Leland & Harste, 1999). There is a wide range of sensitively written materials available about topics such as death, divorce, sexuality, substance abuse, and family violence. Many of these books remain favorites despite their limited use in classrooms.

Factor 3: Conducive Environment

Students in SSR don't just read at their desks—they read everywhere. Comfortable corners with pillows and beanbag chairs appeal to some students. These cozy places encourage students to curl up with a good book. Of course, there aren't enough corners to accommodate every child in the classroom. Most students will choose to read at their desks or at tables around the classroom. However, every student needs a classroom that is quiet and has a minimum of interruptions. Some teachers hang a sign on the outside of their door that announces, "Sshh! We're Reading." Others post rules and expectations designed specifically for SSR. Figure 9.1 was posted in a seventh-grade English classroom.

The topics of some narrative and informational texts may not be desirable for use during a whole class reading; however, these topics are often precisely what students want to read about.

Factor 4: Encouragement

Encouragement comes not in the form of extrinsic rewards like points or grades, but from opportunities to talk about books with peers and teachers. In most successful SSR programs, teachers and students conduct brief book talks to tell others about a book they recommend. In schoolwide SSR efforts, encouragement is also noted in public promotions of reading. At the middle and high school where we work, we feature the monthly reading lists of every staff member, and post pictures of what we're reading on classroom doors. Francois (2015) reported that the middle school principal of the school she studied converted part of his office into a student library of over eight hundred books. The principal also runs a series of book clubs using high-interest texts. The school's efforts to raise the profile of reading resulted in 75 percent of students describing their school as a "reading school" and 72 percent citing opportunities to talk about what they were reading as a primary motivator.

Factor 5: Staff Training

Like all effective instructional practices, SSR efforts are often supported by staff development. Teachers who are introducing SSR to their classrooms can plan procedures, rules, and book rotations between classes. These collegial conversations are also useful for solving problems that may

Figure 9.1 Student and Teacher Expectations for SSR

Student Expectations During SSR	Teacher Expectations During SSR
• Read for the entire SSR period. • Read anything (except textbooks and assigned material). • Respectfully share your thoughts and opinions about what you're reading. We all learn from each other. • Be respectful of others. This means reading quietly. • You may sit or recline wherever you like as long as it does not disturb others. • Please don't ask to leave the room at this time—it disturbs others and shortens your opportunity to read for pleasure.	• I will read silently during the entire period. • I will respectfully share my thoughts and opinions about what I am reading. I learn from you every day. • I will not grade papers or prepare for class during SSR. • I will read for my own pleasure.

arise. At a high school where two of us worked, SSR was a standing agenda item at each professional development session so that teachers could check in with one another.

Factor 6: Nonaccountability

A key feature of SSR is that students are *not* completing logs, writing reflections and book reports, and otherwise doing schoolwork. We have witnessed many programs that violate this principle. The purpose is to build the *habit* of reading, not to assign more work. During the entire SSR session, students read quietly and get lost in their books. That's it. Resist the urge to make it yet another assignment.

Factor 7: Follow-Up Activities

During SSR time, follow-up activities are not projects related to the books students are reading. Instead, students can volunteer to discuss their reading but are not compelled to do so. These conversations typically last five minutes and may be partner conversations, small-group conversations, or whole class dialogues.

Factor 8: Distributed Time to Read

SSR programs occur in regularly scheduled intervals, several times a week. In some cases, they may happen daily. When students anticipate SSR on a regular basis, they fall into the habit of engaging in recreational reading. Remember that what SSR looks like is influenced by the developmental levels of the class. In kindergarten and first grade, SSR is rarely silent and is sustained for only brief periods of time—perhaps ten minutes or so. Younger children are likely to want more, and not less, time to discuss their books after SSR.

Sixth-grade English teacher Frank McCarthy signals to the class that it's time to finish their collaborative tasks. "Three minutes until SSR!" his voice booms. Magazines and paperbacks emerge, and students eye the most coveted spots in the classroom. As five move to the beanbag chairs and floor pillows, Mr. McCarthy continues. "I wanted to do a quick book talk today because I just read this great book over the weekend. It's called *Zulu Dog* [Ferreira, 2002], and it's about a boy named Vusi, who lives in South Africa, and a dog he saves from a leopard attack. One of the things I liked about this book was the way the author wrote about when Vusi finds that the burrow where the dog had been living was attacked. Listen to this:

> When his father has gone, Vusi falls to the ground at
> the entrance by the burrow. The boy stretches his hand
> down the hole and feels nothing but sand. He wants
> to cry, but he refuses to give up hope. He pushes his
> shoulder as far as it will go, trying to reach deeper,
> imagining his arm is an elastic band as he stretches,
> stretches, stretches. His fingers scrabble furiously in the
> dirt at the bottom of the hole, hoping for the touch of
> warm puppy fur. Nothing. [p. 23]

"That's the part that really got me. Anyway, if you like the sound of this book, it'll be over here in the classroom library." Many pairs of eyes follow Mr. McCarthy as he places the book on a shelf. He then pauses to cue up soft instrumental music, a signal that SSR is ready to begin. "You folks know what to do—read quietly, read what you're interested in, and remember, get lost—in a book!" He sets the timer for twenty minutes.

While Mr. McCarthy reads an adult novel, other students are reading a wide variety of texts. Angela is reading *The Skin I'm In* (Flake, 1998), a novel about an African American girl with darker skin who struggles to fit into her peer group. Kimberley is reading the inside cover of *Zulu Dog*, and Marco and Edgar, who have been watching the wildfires in California all week, are poring over the illustrations in a large book called *Disaster! Catastrophes*

That Shook the World (Bonson & Platt, 1997). They are particularly intrigued by the diagrams of the Great Fire of London. Molly has a tablet perched on her knee and is reading an online newspaper from the city she used to live in. After twenty minutes, the timer sounds, and students reluctantly close books and shut down devices. Even Mr. McCarthy tries to read one more sentence as he closes his book. "Does anyone want to talk about what they're reading? Any recommendations?" asks the teacher.

Marco and Edgar, enthusiastic about their disaster book, volunteer to give a book talk.

"We're reading this cool book about disasters like the *Titanic* and the Black Death," says Marco.

"Yeah, today we were looking at the drawings about the Great Fire of London," continues Edgar.

"Would you recommend the book? Why?" reminds Mr. McCarthy.

"Oh, yeah, the best part about it is the drawings. There's all these little facts in there, and you really have to hunt for them," Marco says. "Like how people started killing foreigners while the fire was still going on because they wanted to blame someone. That's just messed up."

After finishing their colorful endorsement of the book, Edgar and Marco, along with the rest of the class, continue with their instructional day. In the meantime, Mr. McCarthy has accomplished several important goals for SSR—building positive attitudes toward reading by emphasizing student choice, creating a supportive environment, providing access to appealing books, and fostering an atmosphere of encouragement. All in all, he and his students have found this to be a great way to spend twenty minutes.

▶ Independent Reading

Like SSR, independent reading is built on a foundation of increasing reading volume and positive attitudes toward reading. However, this instructional approach differs in important ways from SSR. Independent reading is linked to the unit of study and is designed for students to practice the skills they have been learning, as well as to build knowledge about the designated topic. In addition, the teacher is actively engaging with students about their reading. At times, the teacher may be circulating and assisting students with individual instruction, while at other times he or she may be conferring with students about their literacy practices. As part of their independent reading, students share and reflect with peers and the teacher.

The established purpose of the independent reading influences how it is implemented. There are times when we model our thinking for the first few paragraphs of a new reading, then ask students to complete the rest of the article independently. This technique works best when the text is short and can be completed in one class period. However, when the purpose is to build knowledge across a unit of study (often several weeks long), we organize a list of books for students to choose from. The longer texts assigned for independent reading typically require a week or more to complete, and therefore a substantial amount of the reading must be completed outside of class. Therefore, these text lists take into account the range of reading abilities in the class. When students are expected to engage with a text individually, the texts on the list should not all be easy, but they should also not all be so difficult that the student is paralyzed by the task.

The challenge is that when only one text is used, it is not likely to be appropriate for all of the students in a given class at the same moment in time.

The challenge is that when only one text is used, it is not likely to be appropriate for all of the students in a given class at the same moment in time. When teachers assign a whole class book for independent reading, some students struggle and fail while others waste time and get bored. It doesn't matter how good or grade-level appropriate the text is—it will not be a perfect match for every student without instructional interventions. *Shiloh* (Naylor, 1991) is a fantastic book for a lot of students, but we have yet to find an entire class of students who can and want to read that book at the same point in the year. There is nothing in any standards document that says that all of the students have to individually read the same book at the same time.

As noted by McRae and Guthrie's (2009) work on motivation, one way to create a common thread among students who are all reading different texts is through the use of themes or essential questions. A challenge with questions or themes is that they too often give away the information in the text. When they are broad enough to ensure that students see connections between ideas and not so specific that they remove the inquiry for readers, themes and questions can be used to guide text selection matched to the text. For example, when investigating the question, "What is normal, anyway?" different students in an eleventh-grade English class read different books to gain an understanding of some aspect of the issue (see Figure 9.2 for a sample of texts on this topic). They then wrote essays in response to the question, sharing their understanding of the text along the way. This question was not so specific as to ruin the reading or give away the plot.

> **Figure 9.2** Texts That Address the Question,
> "What Is Normal, Anyway?"
>
> ---
>
> Anderson, L. H. *Speak.*
>
> Bauby, J. D. *The Diving Bell and the Butterfly.*
>
> Haddon, M. *The Curious Incident of the Dog in the Night-Time.*
>
> Kesey, K. *One Flew Over the Cuckoo's Nest.*
>
> Morrison, T. *Beloved.*
>
> Porter, R. *Madness: A Brief History.*
>
> Skloot, R. *The Immortal Life of Henrietta Lacks.*
>
> Taylor, J. B. *My Stroke of Insight.*

The key to this approach is to help students find the right independent text. When students are matched with appropriate independent reading texts, they read more complex texts. For example, Genemo selected *My Stroke of Insight* (Taylor, 2008) and learned a great deal about a woman who survived a significant stroke and had to relearn to take care of herself. Seyo selected *The Immortal Life of Henrietta Lacks* (Skloot, 2010) and learned about the woman who donated, without her knowledge, cells that are still used in cancer research today. Abdurashid selected *One Flew Over the Cuckoo's Nest* (Kesey, 1962) and delved into life in a mental hospital. Had the teacher selected one text for all students, none of them would have been as challenged as they were by their independent reading. When we assign whole class readings, we risk undershooting readers and thereby fail to propel them further (Lapp & Fisher, 2009).

▶ Discussing Independent Reading With Students

The teacher is the facilitator of the discussions that occur after independent reading. For example, a third-grade teacher's close reading discussion addressed how the author used vivid language in *Harvesting Hope: The Story of Cesar Chavez* (Krull, 2003). Given that this was a shorter reading, and one the students had read earlier during scaffolded reading, she assigned the remainder of the book to be read independently during the class period. "My focus for this reading was in looking at the author's craft, and I wanted to introduce this concept using a text students were already familiar with," she explained. Students continued to read the picture book and made notes when they found evidence of the technique. When independent reading was finished, the teacher invited discussion about the examples of vivid language in the book. Students offered their observations and furnished evidence using the notes on their comment cards. Meanwhile, the teacher charted their responses on a language chart.

More often, conferring occurs with individual students about their reading. These check-ins are brief (five minutes or so) and can provide a great deal of information about the reader. However, these conferences can limit what readers pay attention to if the questions that are asked do not prompt insightful responses. In other words, the types of questions teachers ask during conferences influence how students read. If they know they're going to get asked a series of recall questions, students will focus their reading on details that will allow them to respond to questions about facts. Alternatively, when asked questions that require evaluation or synthesis, students' reading changes, and they focus their attention on global issues and compare that with their own thinking. The following two examples illustrate this difference.

The types of questions teachers ask during conferences influence how students read.

Over the course of the semester, Morgan had been exclusively asked questions by her English teacher during conferences that required her to recall details and events from *The Hunger Games* (Collins, 2008). For example, she had been asked, "When did the story take place? Where did the story take place? What happened when Katniss first met Gale?" As a result, Morgan became a reader who lacked the critical thinking skills required to respond to the question, "What would it take, in terms of social changes in a society, for a brutal competition like this to occur?" She floundered with that question and instead retold the story line again from the text, unable to connect this story to the content she had learned in her history class.

In another school, Jessie had participated in a number of discussions about texts and had an opportunity to respond to a broader range of questions that tapped into her critical thinking skills. "What might have happened if Peeta had not given Katniss bread? Was there anything that puzzled you in this chapter?" When she was asked the same question about the social changes that could create *The Hunger Games*, Jessie responded with a series of possible events, some based on her extrapolation from the text ("There would probably have been a war"), some from her experience ("I think that the power of government would have to change. I don't think that this could happen in a democracy"), and still others related to her discipline-specific knowledge from her history class ("I can see the link between these games and the ones held at the Colosseum in ancient Rome. It's the idea of 'bread and circuses' to distract the masses from what's really wrong with their government. Even the name of the country—Panem—means 'bread' in Latin. *Panem et circenses*. Bread and circuses. A society has to be willing to give itself over to entertainment rather than pay attention to governance").

▶ Types of Questions Matter in Conferences, Too

Of course, teachers have known about question types and the skills required to answer different types of questions for years. Who hasn't heard of Bloom's Taxonomy (1956) and the levels of knowledge, comprehension, application, analysis, synthesis, and evaluation? We are also interested in the revision of Bloom's Taxonomy for the 21st century (Anderson & Krathwohl, 2001), focusing on the terms *remembering, understanding, applying, analyzing, evaluating*, and *creating*.

But our point here is about questions. What may not be as clear, despite a strong understanding of questioning taxonomies, is the effect repeatedly asking certain kinds of questions can have on the reading habits of students. Over time, when they are asked "lower order" questions, they read for that type of information only. As a cautionary note, we are not suggesting that teachers eliminate remembering, understanding, or applying questions. This information is critical to students' ability to answer complex questions. After all, Jessie would not have been able to answer our question if she hadn't already had a basic understanding of the text. But she also needed to be asked questions that invited her to analyze and evaluate in order to make sophisticated connections using other sources of knowledge to support her claims.

The use of questioning routines such as Question–Answer Relationships (QAR) and Question the Author are effective for developing text-dependent questions for use in conferences. Regardless of the system used, the questions should be developed in advance of the lesson in order to ensure that the discussion regularly guides students back to the reading.

QAR is an instructional strategy designed to teach students how to locate and formulate answers to questions about a reading. The QAR approach "clarifies how students can approach the task of reading texts and answering questions" (Raphael, 1986, p. 517). This is accomplished by teaching about four types of questions. The first two are explicit questions, meaning that the answer can be found in the text. **Right There** questions contain wording that comes directly from the text, with an answer often found in a single sentence. **Think and Search** questions are also derived directly from the text, but the answer must be formulated across more than one sentence. The other two types of questions are implicit, meaning that the answer cannot be located directly in the text, and must be formulated by using what the reader knows as well. **Author and You** is an implicit question that requires the reader to use both information learned in the text and his or her own background knowledge to answer. The final type of implicit question is **On Your Own**, which requires the reader to use prior knowledge to answer. The text may or may not be needed. It is helpful to think of these as "book" and "brain" questions. *Right There* and *Think and Search* are "book" questions because the answers can be found directly in the text. On the other hand, *Author and You* and *On Your Own* are "brain" questions in that readers must consider what they know, as well as what they have learned from the reading. In a close reading, the majority of the questions will be "book" questions. When the teacher is sure that students understand the text, "brain" questions can be used to extend students' learning. See Figure 9.3 for examples of these questions.

Questioning the Author (Beck & McKeown, 2006) requires that students think beyond the words on the page to consider both the author's intent with regard to what he or she has written and his or her degree of success in communicating what was intended. The idea of questioning the author is not an invitation to challenge a writer but rather a way to encourage students to return to the text to find evidence. Students examine the author's intent, craft, clarity, or organization. Questioning the Author focuses on five main questions, and these lend themselves brilliantly to framing questions for conferring about the text a student is reading independently. Over time, students should learn to ask these questions themselves as they read a text. To help them learn how to question an author, teachers can model the types of questions that should be asked of the author by asking students questions, or variations of these questions, as noted in Figure 9.4. Ask students these questions about their independent reading and listen for the depth of their thinking:

1. What is the author trying to tell you?
2. Why is the author telling you that?
3. Does the author say it clearly?

4. How could the author have said things more clearly?

5. What would you say instead?

For example, when April read Annie Davis's August 28, 1864, letter to President Lincoln (Young, 2005) asking if she was a free woman or a slave, her teacher, Hal Bishop, used Questioning the Author to talk with her about her analysis of the letter and the supporting information provided by the author of the book. The text of the letter is not very complex, but the question posed is. As they engaged in a text-based discussion, April focused on the letter and understood that Ms. Davis, the enslaved person, wanted to know if she was legally allowed to leave because she had heard rumor of the Emancipation Proclamation. The teacher and the student also discussed the fact that the book's author stated that because Ms. Davis was

Figure 9.3   Question–Answer Relationships

Question–Answer Relationships		
In the Text (Book Questions)		
Question Type	**Description**	**Question Stems**
Right There	Words in the question and answer are directly stated in the text. It is explicit, and the words or phrases can be found within one sentence.	• How many . . . ? • Who is . . . ? • Where is . . . ? • What is . . . ?
Think and Search	Information is in the text, but readers must think and make connections between passages in the text.	• What is the main idea of . . . ? • What caused . . . ?
In My Head (Brain Questions)		
Question Type	**Description**	**Question Stems**
Author and You	Readers need to think about what they already know, what the author tells them in the text, and how it fits together.	• What is the author implying by . . . ? • What is suggested by . . . ? • What is the author's attitude toward . . . ?
On Your Own	These questions require the reader to use prior knowledge to answer. The text may or may not be needed.	• In your own opinion, . . . ? • Based on your experience, . . . ? • What would you do if . . . ?

Source: Adapted from Fisher, Frey, & Young (2007).

Figure 9.4 Examples of Queries: Initiating,
Follow-Up, and Narrative

Initiating Queries

- What is the author trying to say here?
- What is the author's message?
- What is the author talking about?

Follow-Up Queries

- What does the author mean here?
- Does the author explain this clearly?
- Does this make sense with what the author has told us before?
- How does this connect with what the author has told us before?
- Does the author tell us why?
- Why do you think the author tells us this now?

Narrative Queries

- How do things look for this character now?
- How has the author let you know that something has changed?
- How has the author settled this for us?
- Given what the author has already told us about this character, what do you think he's up to?

Source: Beck, McKeown, Hamilton, & Kucan (1997).

from Maryland, a border state that was not in rebellion against the United States, the proclamation did not apply to her. They agreed that Ms. Davis's letter was clear but that the Emancipation Proclamation was confusing and misled a lot of people. Mr. Bishop's use of the Questioning the Author protocol to shape his discussion with April helped her to connect the content of the primary source document to the supporting information written by the book's author.

▶ Conclusion

This book has focused on text complexity across a number of dimensions, including quantitative factors, qualitative values, and task considerations.

Teachers have to understand what makes a text complex so that they can develop students' understanding of those texts. In addition, teachers should plan a wide range of teacher-led, peer-led, and independent tasks that allow students to develop their reading habits. We believe that all students can read more, and better, than they do today. We have to collectively raise our expectations, and the associated instructional scaffolds, if students are to be successful in their adult lives. Literacy is a game changer, and we should be reminded that students who can read but don't are no better off than those who cannot read. Our role, as teachers, is to develop lifelong readers who choose to read and, beyond that, who choose to read *widely*—seeking out and devouring texts that are (and are not) complex, for information and enjoyment.

References

Adler, M. J. (1940). *How to read a book*. New York, NY: Touchstone.

Adler, M. J., & Van Doren, C. (1972). *How to read a book* (3rd ed.). New York, NY: Touchstone.

Afflerbach, P., Pearson, P. D., & Paris, S. (2008). Clarifying differences between reading skills and reading strategies. *The Reading Teacher, 61*, 364–373.

Aguilar, D. (2013). *Space encyclopedia: A tour of our solar system*. Washington, DC: National Geographic Kids.

Alexander, P. A. Schallert, D. L., & Hare, V. C. (1991). Coming to terms: How researchers in learning and literacy talk about knowledge. *Review of Educational Research, 61*(3), 315–343.

Ali, N., & Minoui, D. (2010). *I am Nujood, age 10 and divorced* (L. Cloverdale, Trans.). New York, NY: Broadway.

Aliki. (1997). *My visit to the zoo*. New York, NY: HarperCollins.

Allington, R. L., & Cunningham, P. M. (2007). *Schools that work: Where all children read and write*. Boston, MA: Pearson.

Altieri, J. L. (2011). *Content counts! Developing disciplinary literacy skills, K–6*. Newark, DE: International Reading Association.

American Library Association. (2008). *Caldecott medal terms and criteria*. Retrieved from http://www.ala.org/alsc/awardsgrants/bookmedia/caldecottmedal/caldecottterms/caldecottterms

Anderson, L. H. (2011). *Speak*. New York, NY: Square Fish.

Anderson, L. W., & Krathwohl, D. R. (Eds.). (2001). *A taxonomy for learning, teaching and assessing: A revision of Bloom's Taxonomy of educational objectives: Complete edition*. New York, NY: Longman.

Anderson, R. C., Hiebert, E. H., Scott, J. A., & Wilkinson, I. A. G. (1985). *Becoming a nation of readers: The report of the Commission on Reading*. Champaign, IL: Center for the Study of Reading, National Institute of Education, National Academy of Education.

Anderson, R. C., Wilson, P. T., & Fielding, L. G. (1988). Growth in reading and how children spend their time outside school. *Reading Research Quarterly, 23*, 285–303.

Armbruster, B. B. (1996). Considerate texts. In D. Lapp, J. Flood, & N. Farnan (Eds.), *Content area reading and learning: Instructional strategies* (pp. 47–58). Boston, MA: Allyn & Bacon.

Austen, J., & Winters, B. E. (2009). *Sense and sensibility and sea monsters.* Philadelphia, PA: Quirk.

awetblackbough. (2010, July 25). Langston Hughes reads "The Negro Speaks of Rivers" [YouTube video]. Retrieved from https://www.youtube.com/watch?v=5mFp40WJbsA

Bailin, A., & Grafstein, A. (2001). The linguistic assumptions underlying readability formulae: A critique. *Language & Communication, 21,* 285–301.

Bakken, J. P., & Whedon, C. K. (2002). Teaching text structure to improve reading comprehension. *Intervention in School and Clinic, 37*(4), 229–233.

Baldwin, J. (1965). Sonny's blues. Reprinted from *Going to meet the man.* New York, NY: Vintage.

Bardoe, C. (2006). *Gregor Mendel: The friar who grew peas.* New York, NY: Harry N. Abrams.

Barone, D., & Barone, R. (2015, June). *An insider view of the standards.* Session at the 36th Annual San Diego State University Reading and Language Arts Conference, San Diego, CA.

Bauby, J. D. (1998). *The diving bell and the butterfly.* New York, NY: Vintage.

Beck, I. L., & McKeown, M. G. (2006). *Improving comprehension with questioning the author: A fresh and enhanced view of a proven approach.* New York, NY: Scholastic.

Beck, I. L., McKeown, M. G., Hamilton, R. L., & Kucan, L. (1997). *Questioning the author: An approach for enhancing student engagement with text.* Newark, DE: International Reading Association.

Beck, I. L., McKeown, M. G., Omanson, R. C., & Pople, M. T. (1984). Improving the comprehensibility of stories: The effects of revisions that improve coherence. *Reading Research Quarterly, 19*(3), 263–277.

Becklake, S. (1998). *All about space.* New York, NY: Scholastic.

Beeler, S. B. (1998). *Throw your tooth on the roof: Tooth traditions from around the world.* New York, NY: Houghton Mifflin.

Betts, E. A. (1946). *Foundations of reading instruction with emphasis on differentiated guidance.* New York, NY: American Book Company.

Blau, S. (1994). Transactions between theory and practice in the teaching of literature. In J. Flood & J. Langer (Eds.), *Literature instruction: Practice and policy* (pp. 19–52). New York, NY: Leadership, Policy, and Research Series, Scholastic Press.

Bloom, B. S. (1956). *Taxonomy of educational objectives: The classification of educational goals: Handbook I, cognitive domain.* New York, NY: Longman.

Bogacki, T. (1996). *Cat and mouse.* New York, NY: Farrar, Straus & Giroux.

Bonson, R., & Platt, R. (1997). *Disaster! Catastrophes that shook the world.* New York, NY: DK Publishing.

Boscolo, P., & Mason, L. (2003). Topic knowledge, text coherence, and interest: How they interact in learning from instructional texts. *Journal of Experimental Education, 71*(2), 126–148.

Boyce, J. (2006). *Boy in the striped pajamas.* New York, NY: Random House.

Brann, E. T. H. (1989). *Paradoxes of education in a republic.* Chicago, IL: University of Chicago.

Branzei, S. (2002). *Grossology: The science of really gross things.* New York, NY: Price Stern Sloan.

Browne, A. (1998). *Voices in the park.* New York, NY: DK Publishing.

Butler-Bowdon, T. (2007). *50 psychology classics: Who we are, how we think, what we do.* Boston, MA: Nicholas Brealey.

Cervetti, G. N., & Hiebert, E. H. (2015). The sixth pillar of reading instruction: Knowledge development. *The Reading Teacher, 68*(7), 548–551.

Chall, J. S., Bissex, G., Conard, S. S., & Harris-Sharples, S. (1996). *Qualitative assessment of text difficulty: A practical guide for teachers and writers.* Cambridge, MA: Brookline Books.

Chall, J. S., & Dale, E. (1995). *Manual for the new Dale-Chall readability formula.* Cambridge, MA: Brookline.

Chekhov, A. (2012). An upheaval. *The lady with the dog and other stories.* Seattle, WA: Create Space. (Original work published 1917)

Ciardi, J. (1987). *You read to me, I'll read to you.* New York, NY: Harper Trophy.

Ciardiello, A. V. (2002). Helping adolescents understand cause/effect text structure in social studies. *Social Studies, 93*(1), 31–36.

Cisneros, S. (1991). *Women hollering creek and other stories.* New York, NY: Vintage.

Clark, A., Anderson, R. C., Kuo, L., Kim, I., Archodidou, A., & Nguyen-Jahiel, K. (2003). Collaborative reasoning: Expanding ways for children to talk and think in school. *Educational Psychology Review, 15*(2), 181–198.

Cohen, S. A., & Steinberg, J. E. (1983). Effects of three types of vocabulary on readability of intermediate grade science textbooks: An application of Finn's transfer feature theory. *Reading Research Quarterly, 19*(1), 86–101.

Coles, R. (1995). *The story of Ruby Bridges*. New York, NY: Scholastic.

Collins, S. (2008). *The hunger games*. New York, NY: Scholastic.

Creech, S. (2001). *Love that dog*. New York, NY: HarperCollins.

Cromley, J. G., & Azevedo, R. (2007). Testing and refining the direct and inferential mediation model of reading comprehension. *Journal of Educational Psychology, 99*(2), 311–325.

Cronin, D. (2000). *Click, clack, moo: Cows that type*. New York, NY: Classic Boar Books, Simon & Schuster.

Cross, D. R., & Paris, S. G. (1988). Developmental and instructional analyses of children's metacognition and reading comprehension. *Journal of Educational Psychology, 80*(2), 131–142.

Crossley, S. A., Dufty, D. F., McCarthy, P. M., & McNamara, D. S. (2007). Toward a new readability: A mixed model approach. In D. S. McNamara & G. Trafton (Eds.), *Proceedings of the 29th annual conference of the Cognitive Science Society* (pp. 197–202). Cognitive Science Society.

Cullinan, B .E. (1989). *Literature and the child* (2nd ed.). San Diego, CA: Harcourt Brace Jovanovich.

Curtis, C. P. (1995). *The Watsons go to Birmingham—1963*. New York, NY: Bantam Doubleday Dell Books for Young Readers.

Dale, E., & O'Rourke, J. (1976). *The living word vocabulary, the words we know: A national vocabulary inventory*. Elgin, IL: Dome.

Davison, A., & Kantor, R. N. (1982). On the failure of readability formulas to define readable texts: A case study from adaptations. *Reading Research Quarterly, 27*(4), 187–209.

Daywalt, D. (2013). *The day the crayons quit*. New York, NY: Penguin.

Dendy, L., & Boring, M. (2005). *Guinea pig scientists: Bold self-experimenters in science and medicine*. New York, NY: Holt.

Denenberg, D., & Roscoe, L. (2001). *50 American heroes every kid should meet*. Brookfield, CT: Millbrook Press.

dePaola, T. (1999). *26 Fairmount Avenue*. New York, NY: G. P. Putnam's Sons.

Donovan, M. S., & Bransford, J. D. (Eds.). (2005). *How students learn: History, mathematics, and science in the classroom*. Washington, DC: National Academies Press.

Duffy, G. G. (2003). *Explaining reading: A resource for teaching concepts, skill, and strategies*. New York, NY: Guilford.

Duke, N. K. (2000). 3.6 minutes per day: The scarcity of informational texts in first grade. *Reading Research Quarterly, 35*, 202–224.

Dunn, M. W. (2011). Writing-skills instruction: Teachers' perspectives about effective practices. *Journal of Reading Education, 37*(1), 18–25.

Elliott, S. N. (2015). Measuring opportunity to learn and achievement growth: Key research issues with implications for the effective education of all students. *Remedial & Special Education, 36*(1), 58–64.

Ellis, D. (2009). *The breadwinner.* Berkeley, CA: Groundwood Books.

Empson, W. (1930). *Seven types of ambiguity.* London, UK: Chatto & Windus.

Ericsson, K. A., & Charness, N. (1994). Expert performance: Its structure and acquisition. *American Psychologist, 49*(8), 725–747.

Ericsson, K. A., Krampe, R. T., & Tesch-Römer, C. (1993). The role of deliberate practice in the acquisition of expert performance. *Psychological Review, 100*(3), 363–406.

Evans, L. (2011). *Moon power.* New York, NY: Scholastic.

Ferreira, A. (2002). *Zulu dog.* New York, NY: Frances Foster.

Fisher, D., & Frey, N. (2009). *Background knowledge: The missing piece of the comprehension puzzle.* Portsmouth, NH: Heinemann.

Fisher, D., & Frey, N. (2010). *Guided instruction: How to develop confident and successful learners.* Alexandria, VA: ASCD.

Fisher, D., & Frey, N. (2011). *The purposeful classroom: How to structure lessons with learning goals in mind.* Alexandria, VA: ASCD.

Fisher, D., & Frey, N. (2013). Reading and reasoning: Fostering comprehension across multiple texts. *Engaging the Adolescent Learner IRA E-ssentials.*

Fisher, D., Frey, N., Anderson, H., & Thayre, M. (2014). *Text dependent questions: Pathways to close and critical reading.* Thousand Oaks, CA: Corwin Literacy.

Fisher, D., Frey, N., & Lapp, D. (2008a). *In a reading state of mind: Brain research, teacher modeling, and comprehension instruction.* Newark, DE: International Reading Association.

Fisher, D., Frey, N., & Lapp, D. (2008b). Shared readings: Modeling comprehension, vocabulary, text structures, and text features for older readers. *The Reading Teacher, 61,* 548–557.

Fisher, D., Frey, N., & Lapp, D. (2011). Coaching middle-level teachers to think aloud improves comprehension instruction and student reading achievement. *The Teacher Educator, 46,* 231–243.

Fisher, D., Frey, N., & Young, L. (2007). *After school content literacy project for California.* Sacramento: California Department of Education.

Flake, S. G. (1998). *The skin I'm in.* New York, NY: Hyperion.

Fleischman, J. (2002) *Phineas Gage: A gruesome but true story about brain science*. New York, NY: Houghton Mifflin.

Foer, J. S. (2005). *Extremely loud and incredibly close*. New York, NY: Houghton Mifflin.

Fountas, I. C., & Pinnell, G. S. (1999). *Matching books to readers: Using leveled books in guided reading, K–3*. Portsmouth, NH: Heinemann.

Francis, W. N., & Kucera, H. (1964). *Brown corpus manual: Manual of information to accompany* A standard corpus of present-day edited American English, for use with digital computers. Providence, RI: Brown University Department of Linguistics.

Francois, C. (2015). An urban school shapes young adolescents' motivation to read. *Voices from the Middle, 23*(1), 68–72.

Frey, N., Fisher, D., & Berkin, A. (2009). *Good habits, great readers: Building the literacy community*. Upper Saddle River, NJ: Merrill Education.

Frey, N., Fisher, D., & Everlove, S. (2009). *Productive group work: How to engage students, build teamwork, and promote understanding*. Alexandria, VA: ASCD.

Freytag, G. (1863). *Die technik des dramas*. Lepizig, Germany: S. Hirzel.

Frost, R. (2011). Nothing gold can stay. In P. Janeczko (Ed.), *Poetry in the middle grades* (p. 180). Portsmouth, NH: Heinemann. (Original work published 1923)

Fry, E. (2002). Readability versus leveling. *The Reading Teacher, 56*(3), 286–291.

Gallant, R. (1997). *Sand on the move: The story of dunes*. New York, NY: Grolier.

Ganeri, A. (2009). *Body basics: Bones*. New York, NY: Scholastic.

Geisel, T. S. [Dr. Seuss]. (1957). *How the Grinch stole Christmas*. New York, NY: Random House.

Geisel, T. S. [Dr. Seuss]. (1958). *"Yertle the Turtle" and other stories*. New York, NY: Random House.

Geisel, T. S. [Dr. Seuss]. (1961). *"The Sneetches" and other stories*. New York, NY: Random House.

Geisel, T. S. [Dr. Seuss]. (1971). *The Lorax*. New York, NY: Random House.

Gibbons, G. (1991). *Zoo*. New York, NY: HarperCollins.

Gibbons, G. (1993). *From seed to plant*. New York, NY: Holiday House.

Gibbons, G. (2011). *It's snowing*. New York, NY: Holiday House.

Gibbs, W. W. (2003). Untangling the roots of cancer. *Scientific American*. Retrieved from http://www.scientificamerican.com/article/untangling-the-roots-of-c-2003-07/

Golding, W. (1959). *Lord of the flies.* New York, NY: Capricorn Books.

Graesser, A. C., McNamara, D. S., & Kulikowich, J. M. (2011). Coh-Metrix: Providing multilevel analyses of text characteristics. *Educational Researcher, 40*(5), 223–234.

Graesser, A. C., McNamara, D. S., & Louwerse, M. M. (2011). Methods of automated text analysis. In M. L. Kamil, P. D. Pearson, E. B. Moje, & P. P. Afflerbach (Eds.), *Handbook of reading research,* (Vol. IV, pp. 34–53). New York, NY: Routledge.

Gray, T. (2009). *The elements: A visual exploration of every known atom in the universe.* New York, NY: Black Dog & Leventhal.

Gray, W. S., & Leary, B. (1935). *What makes a book readable.* Chicago, IL: University of Chicago Press.

Gulbin, S. (1966). Parallels and contrast in *Lord of the flies* and *Animal farm. English Journal, 55*(1), 86–88, 92.

Gunning, T. G. (2003). The role of readability in today's classrooms. *Topics in Language Disorders, 23,* 175–189.

Haddon, M. (2003). *The curious incident of the dog in the night-time.* New York, NY: Doubleday.

Hakim, J. (2005). *A history of US: The first Americans* (Book 1, 3rd ed.). New York, NY: Oxford University Press.

Halladay, J. (2012). Revisiting key assumptions of the reading level framework. *Reading Teacher, 66*(1), 53–62.

Halliday, M. A. K. (1985). *Spoken and written language.* Oxford, UK: Oxford University Press.

Hansten, P. D., & Horn, J. R. (2014). *Drug interactions analysis and management 2014* (9th ed.). St. Louis, MO: Lippincott Williams & Wilkins.

Harvey, C. A. (2011). An inside view of Lexile measures: An interview with Malbert Smith III. *Knowledge Quest, 39*(4), 56–59.

Hasbrouck, J., & Tindal, G. A. (2006). Oral reading fluency norms: A valuable assessment tool for reading teachers. *Reading Teacher, 59*(7), 636–644.

Haston, W. (2007). Teacher modeling as an effective teaching strategy. *Music Educators Journal, 93*(4), 26–30.

Hemingway, E. (1998). Hills like white elephants. *The complete short stories of Ernest Hemingway* (pp. 211–214). New York, NY: Scribner. (Original work published 1927)

Hendy, H. M., & Raudenbush, B. (2000). Effectiveness of teacher modeling to encourage food acceptance in preschool children. *Appetite, 34,* 61–76.

Hesse, H. (2011). *Siddhartha*. New York, NY: Simon & Brown. (Original work published 1922)

Hiebert, E. H. (2011). *Using multiple sources of information in establishing text complexity*. Reading Research Report #11.03. Retrieved from http://textproject .org/research/reading-research-reports/a-case-for-using-multiple-sources-of-information-in-establishing-text-complexity/

Hiebert, E. H., & Martin, L. A. (2001). The texts of beginning instruction. In S. B. Neuman & D. K. Dickinson (Eds.), *Handbook of early literacy research* (pp. 361–376). New York, NY: Guilford.

Hill, L. C. (2004). *Harlem stomp! A cultural history of the Harlem Renaissance*. New York, NY: Little, Brown Books for Young Readers.

History Matters. (n.d.). "A date which will live in infamy": FDR asks for a declaration of war [Recording of Roosevelt's day of infamy speech]. Retrieved from http://historymatters.gmu.edu/d/5166

Howard, R. W. (2003). The shrinking of social studies. *Social Education, 67*, 285–288.

Huggins-Cooper, L. (2008). *Awesome animals: Beastly birds and bats*. New York, NY: Scholastic.

Hughes, L. (2015). The weary blues. In *The weary blues* (pp. 5–6). New York, NY: Knopf. (Original work published 1926)

Innocenti, R. (1985). *Rose Blanche*. Mankato, MN: Creative Editions.

Institute of Education Sciences. (2010, September). *Adolescent literacy: Reciprocal teaching* [What Works Clearinghouse intervention report]. Washington, DC: U.S. Department of Education. Retrieved from http://ies.ed.gov/ncee/wwc/ interventionreport.aspx?sid=434

Ipcizade, C. (2008). *'Twas the day before Zoo Day*. Mt. Pleasant, SC: Sylvan Dell.

Ivey, G., & Johnston, P. (2013). Engagement with young adult literature: Processes and outcomes. *Reading Research Quarterly, 48*(3), 1–21.

Jackson, T. (2010). *Micromonsters: Creatures that live on your skin, in your hair, and in your home!* New York, NY: Sandy Creek.

Joos, M. (1967). *Five clocks*. New York, NY: Harcourt.

Juel, D. (1998). *Messianic exegesis: Christological interpretation of the Old Testament in early Christianity*. Minneapolis, MN: Fortress Press.

Just, M. A., & Carpenter, P. A. (1992). A capacity theory of comprehension: Individual differences in working memory. *Psychological Review, 99*, 122–149.

Justice, L. M., Pullen, P. C., & Pence, K. (2008). Influence of verbal and nonverbal references to print on preschoolers' visual attention to print during storybook reading. *Developmental Psychology, 44*(3), 855–866.

Kamkwanba, W., & Mealer, B. (2012). *The boy who harnessed the wind.* New York, NY: Dial.

Kapur, M. (2008). Productive failure. *Cognition and Instruction, 26*(3), 379–424.

Kesey, K. (1962). *One flew over the cuckoo's nest.* New York, NY: Viking Press.

Kintsch, W. (1974). *The representation of meaning in memory.* Hillsdale, NJ: Erlbaum.

Kintsch, W., & Van Dijk, T. A. (1978). Toward a model of text comprehension and production. *Psychological Review, 85*(5), 363–394.

Kipling, R. (1985). *The jungle book.* New York, NY: Bantam. (Original work published 1894)

Kobayashi, M. (2002). Method effects on reading comprehension test performance: Text organization and response format. *Language Testing, 19*, 193–220.

Koegel, T. (2010). *The exceptional presenter goes virtual: Take command of your message, create an "in-person" experience, and captivate any remote audience.* Austin, TX: Greenleaf Book Group Press.

Konigsburg, E. L. (1967). *From the mixed-up files of Mrs. Basil E. Frankweiler.* Konigsburg, NY: Atheneum Books.

Kontovourki, S. (2012). Reading leveled books in assessment-saturated classrooms: A close examination of unmarked processes of assessment. *Reading Research Quarterly, 47*(2), 153–171.

Koslin, B. L., Zeno, S., & Koslin, S. (1987). *The DRP: An effective measure of reading.* New York, NY: College Entrance Examination Board.

Kristo, J. V., & Bamford, R. A. (2004). *Nonfiction in focus: A comprehensive framework for helping students become independent readers and writers of nonfiction, K–6.* New York, NY: Scholastic.

Krull, K. (2003). *Harvesting hope: The story of Cesar Chavez.* New York, NY: HMH Books for Young Readers.

Kush, J. C., & Watkins, M. W. (1996). Long-term stability of children's attitudes toward reading. *Journal of Educational Research, 89*, 315–319.

Ladson-Billings, G. (2006). Yes, but how do we do it? Practicing culturally relevant pedagogy. In J. Landsman & C. W. Lewis (Eds.), *White teachers/diverse classrooms: A guide to building inclusive schools, promoting high expectations and eliminating racism* (pp. 29–42). Sterling, VA: Stylus.

Landauer, T. K., Kireyev, K., & Panaccione, C. (2011). World maturity: A new metric for word knowledge. *Scientific Studies of Reading, 15*, 92–108.

Landauer, T., McNamara, D. S., Dennis, S., & Kintsch, W. (Eds.). (2007). *Handbook of latent semantic analysis*. Mahwah, NJ: Erlbaum.

Lapp, D., & Fisher, D. (2009). It's all about the book: Motivating teens to read. *Journal of Adolescent & Adult Literacy, 52*(7), 556–651.

Lapp, D., Fisher, D., & Grant, M. (2008). "You can read this text—I'll show you how": Interactive comprehension instruction. *Journal of Adolescent & Adult Literacy, 51*, 372–382.

Leland, C., & Harste, J. (1999). Is this appropriate for children? Books that bring realistic social issues into the classroom. *Practically Primary, 4*(3), 4–6.

Leon, V. (2001). *Uppity women of the new world*. New York, NY: MJF Books.

Lesaux, N. K., & Kiefer, M. J. (2010). Exploring sources of reading comprehension difficulties among language minority learners and their classmates in early adolescence. *American Educational Research Journal, 47*(3), 596–632.

Liebman, D. (2003). *I want to be a zookeeper*. Buffalo, NY: Firefly.

Madison, D. (1814, August 23). Letter to Anna Payne on the burning of Washington, DC. Retrieved from http://www.nationalcenter.org/Washington Burning1814.html

Maestro, B. (1995). *The story of money*. New York, NY: HarperCollins Mulberry.

Maloch, B., & Horsey, M. (2013). Living inquiry: Learning from and about informational texts in a second-grade classroom. *The Reading Teacher, 66*, 475–485.

Marschall, K. (1997). *Inside the* Titanic. New York, NY: Madison Press Books.

Martel, Y. (2001). *Life of Pi*. Boston, MA: Houghton Mifflin Harcourt.

McCracken, R. A. (1971). Initiating sustained silent reading. *Journal of Reading, 14*, 521–524, 582–583.

McNamara, D. S., & Kintsch, W. (1996). Learning from text: Effects of prior knowledge and text coherence. *Discourse Processes, 22*, 247–288.

McRae, A., & Guthrie, J. T. (2009). Promoting reasons for reading: Teacher practices that impact motivation. In E. H. Hiebert (Ed.), *Reading more, reading better* (pp. 55–76). New York, NY: Guilford.

McVay, J. C., & Kane, M. J. (2011). Why does working memory capacity predict variation in reading comprehension? On the influence of mind wandering and executive attention [Electronic version]. *Journal of Experimental Psychology: General*. Retrieved from psycnet.apa.org/psycinfo/2011–19417–001/

Mesmer, H. A. E. (2007). *Tools for matching readers to texts: Research-based practices*. New York, NY: Guilford.

Meyer, B. J. F. (2003). Text coherence and readability. *Topics in Language Disorders, 23*, 204–224.

Michaels, S., O'Connor, C., & Resnick, L. (2008). Deliberative discourse idealized and realized: Accountable talk in the classroom and in civic life. *Studies in Philosophy and Education, 27*(4), 283–297.

Mikaelsen, B. (1998). *Petey*. New York, NY: Hyperion Books for Children.

Moline, S. (2012). *I see what you mean: Visual literacy K–8* (2nd ed.). Portland, ME: Stenhouse.

Moll, L. (1992). Funds of knowledge for teaching: Using a qualitative approach to connect homes and classrooms. *Theory Into Practice, 31*(2), 132–141.

Morgan, A., Wilcox, B. R., & Eldredge, J. L. (2000). Effect of difficulty levels on second-grade delayed readers using dyad reading. *Journal of Educational Research, 94*, 113–119.

Morley, J. (2002). *You wouldn't want to be an American pioneer! A wilderness you'd rather not tame*. Danbury, CT: Franklin Watts.

Morrison, T. (2004). *Beloved*. New York, NY: Vintage.

Murray, L. (2010). *Breaking night: A memoir of forgiveness, survival, and my journey from homelessness to Harvard*. New York, NY: Hatchette.

National Center for Education Statistics. (2013). *The nation's report card: A first look: 2013 mathematics and reading* (NCES 2014–451). Washington, DC: Institute of Education Sciences, U.S. Department of Education.

National Governors Association Center for Best Practices & Council of Chief State School Officers. (2010a). *Common Core State Standards*. Washington, DC: Authors.

National Governors Association Center for Best Practices & Council of Chief State School Officers. (2010b). *Common Core State Standards for English language arts & literacy in history/social studies, science, and technical subjects—Appendix A: Research supporting key elements of the standards, Glossary of key terms*. Retrieved from http://www.corestandards.org/assets/Appendix_A.pdf

National Governors Association & Council of Chief State School Officers. (n.d.) *Supplemental information for Appendix A of the Common Core State Standards for English Language Arts and Literacy: New research on text complexity*. Retrieved from http://www.corestandards.org/assets/E0813_Appendix_A_New_Research_on_Text_Complexity.pdf.

National Institute of Child Health and Human Development. (2000). Report of the National Reading Panel: *Teaching children to read: An evidence-based assessment of the scientific research literature on reading and its implications for reading instruction* (NIH Publication No. 00–4769). Washington, DC: U.S. Government Printing Office.

Naylor, P. R. (1991). *Shiloh*. New York, NY: Bantam Doubleday Dell.

Newman, P. (2014). *Plastic, ahoy! Investigating the great Pacific garbage patch*. Minneapolis, MN: Millbrook Press.

Orwell, G. (1946). *Animal farm.* New York, NY: Harcourt, Brace.

Palincsar, A. S., & Brown, A. L. (1986). Interactive teaching to promote independent learning from text. *The Reading Teacher, 39*(8), 771–777.

Paris, S. G. (2005). Reinterpreting the development of reading skills. *Reading Research Quarterly, 40*(2), 184–202.

Parsons, L. (2001). Exploring the functional neuroanatomy of music performance, perception, and comprehension. In R. Zatorre & I. Peretz (Eds.), *The biological foundations of music* (pp. 211–230). New York: New York Academy of Sciences (Vol. 930).

Pearson, P. D. (2013). Research foundations of the Common Core State Standards in English language arts. In Susan B. Neumann & Linda B. Gambrell (Eds.), *Quality reading instruction in the age of Common Core Standards* (pp. 237–262). Newark, DE: International Reading Association.

Pearson, P. D., & Hiebert, E. H. (2014). The state of the field: Qualitative analyses of text complexity. *Elementary School Journal, 115*(2), 161–183.

Pennell, C. (2014). In the age of analytic reading. *Reading Teacher, 68*(4), 251–260.

Piaget, J. (1974). *The language and thought of the child.* New York, NY: Meridian.

Pilgreen, J. L. (2000). *The SSR handbook: How to organize and manage a sustained silent reading program.* Portsmouth, NH: Boynton/Cook.

Poe, E. A. (1988). *Marginalia.* Charlottesville: University of Virginia. (Original work published 1844)

Poe, E. A. (2002). The tell-tale heart. In *Edgar Allan Poe: Complete tales and poems* (pp. 199–202). Edison, NJ: Castle Books. (Original work published 1843)

Porter, R. (2003). *Madness: A brief history.* New York, NY: Oxford University Press.

Powell, W. R., & Dunkeld, C. G. (1971). Validity of the IRI reading levels. *Elementary English, 48,* 637–642.

Quindlen, A. (2001, September 27). A quilt of a country. *Newsweek.*

RAND Reading Study Group. (2002). *Reading for understanding: Toward an R&D program in reading comprehension.* Santa Monica, CA: RAND.

Rankine, C. (2015, June 22). The condition of black life is one of mourning. *The New York Times.* Retrieved from http://www.nytimes.com/2015/06/22/maga zine/the-condition-of-black-life-is-one-of-mourning.html?_r=0

Raphael, T. E. (1986). Teaching children question-answer relationships, revisited. *The Reading Teacher, 39,* 516–522.

Raphael, T. E., & Au, K. H. (2005). QAR: Enhancing comprehension and test taking across grades and content areas. *The Reading Teacher, 59,* 207–221.

Raschka, C. (1993). *Yo! Yes?* New York, NY: Orchard Books.

Raschka, C. (2000). *Ring! Yo?* New York, NY: Dorling Kindersley.

Regan, K., & Berkeley, S. (2012). Effective reading and writing instruction: A focus on modeling. *Intervention in School and Clinic, 47*(5), 276–282.

Richards, R. I. (1929). *Practical criticism: A study of literary judgment.* London, UK: Routledge & Kegan Paul.

Ring, S. (2002). *Blood.* New York, NY: Newbridge Educational Publishing.

Romaine, S. (1994). *Language in society: An introduction to sociolinguistics.* New York, NY: Oxford University Press.

Roop, P., & Roop, C. (2011). *Baby dolphin's first day.* New York, NY: Sterling.

Rose, D., & Martin, J. R. (2012). *Learning to write, reading to learn: Genre, knowledge and pedagogy in the Sydney school.* Sheffield, UK: Equinox.

Rosenblatt, L. M. (1978). *The reader, the text, the poem: The transactional theory of literary work.* Carbondale: Southern Illinois.

Rosenblatt, L. (1995). *Literature as exploration* (5th ed.). New York, NY: Modern Language Association of America.

Rosenblatt, L. M. (2003). Literary theory. In J. Flood, D. Lapp, J. R. Squire, & J. M. Jensen (Eds.), *Handbook of research on teaching the English language arts* (2nd ed., pp. 67–73). Mahwah, NJ: Erlbaum.

Ross, D., Fisher, D., & Frey, N. (2009). The art of argumentation. *Science and Children, 47*(3), 28–31.

Roth, P. (1994). *Portnoy's complaint.* New York, NY: Random House. (Original work published 1969)

Sachar, L. (1998). *Holes.* New York: Farrar, Straus & Giroux.

Salinger, J. D. (1951). *The catcher in the rye.* New York, NY: Modern Library.

School Renaissance Institute. (2000). *The ATOS readability formula for books and how it compares to other formulas.* Retrieved from www.windsorct.org/sagelmc/ReadabilityComparisonArticle.pdf

Schwartz, J. (2007, March 11). Sunday book review of children's books: *The Invention of Hugo Cabret. The New York Times.* Retrieved at http://www.nytimes.com/2007/03/11/books/review/Schwartz.t.html?_r=0

Seda, M. M., Liguori, O. Z., & Seda, C. M. (1999, Autumn). Bridging literacy and social studies: Engaging prior knowledge through children's books. *TESOL, 8,* 34–40.

Shakespeare, W. (1997). As you like it. In *The complete works of Shakespeare* [Wordsworth Royals Series]. London, UK: Wordsworth Editions. (Original work published 1599)

Shanahan, C., & Shanahan, T. (2014). Does disciplinary literacy have a place in elementary school? *The Reading Teacher, 67,* 636–639.

Shanahan, T. (2011, August 21). Rejecting instructional level theory. *Shanahan on Literacy.* Retrieved from http://www.shanahanonliteracy.com/2011/08/rejecting-instructional-level-theory.html

Shanahan, T., & Shanahan, C. (2008). Teaching disciplinary literacy to adolescents: Rethinking content-area literacy. *Harvard Educational Review, 78*(1), 40–59.

Silverman, H. M. (2012). *The pill book* (15th ed.). New York, NY: Bantam.

Singer, M. (1995). *A wasp is not a bee.* New York, NY: Scholastic.

Skloot, R. (2010). *The immortal life of Henrietta Lacks.* New York, NY: Crown.

Skouge, J. R., Rao, K., & Boisvert, P. C. (2007). Promoting early literacy for diverse learners using audio and video technology. *Early Childhood Education Journal, 35*(1), 5–11.

Sloan, C. (2002). *Bury the dead: Tombs, corpses, mummies, skeletons, and rituals.* Washington, DC: National Geographic.

Smith, D., Stenner, A. J., Horabin, I., & Smith, M. (1989). *The Lexile scale in theory and practice: Final report* [ERIC Document Reproduction Service No. ED 307577]. Washington, DC: MetaMetrics.

Smith, J. (2004). *Bone: One volume edition.* New York, NY: Scholastic Cartoon Books.

Snow, C. E., Burns, M. S., & Griffin, R. (1998). *Preventing reading difficulty in young children.* Washington, DC: National Academies Press.

Stahl, S. A., & Heubach, K. M. (2005). Fluency-oriented reading instruction. *Journal of Literacy Research, 37,* 25–60.

Steinbeck, J. (2006). *The grapes of wrath.* New York, NY: Penguin Classics. (Original work published 1939)

Stricht, T. G., & James, J. H. (1984). Listening and reading. In P. D. Pearson, R. Barr, M. L. Kamil, & P. Mosenthal (Eds.), *Handbook of reading research* (Vol. 1, pp. 293–317). White Plains, NY: Longman.

Taback, S. (1997). *There was an old lady who swallowed a fly.* New York, NY: Viking.

Taylor, J. B. (2008). *My stroke of insight.* New York, NY: Viking.

Terkel, S. (1974). *Working: People talk about what they do all day and how they feel about what they do.* New York, NY: Pantheon Books.

Thomas, H. K., Healy, A. F., & Greenberg, S. N. (2007). Familiarization effects for bilingual letter detection involving translation or exact text repetition. *Canadian Journal of Experimental Psychology, 61*(4), 304–315.

Tomlinson, C. A., & Imbeau, M. B. (2010). *Leading and managing a differentiated classroom.* Alexandria, VA: ASCD.

Tsuchiya, Y. (1951). *Faithful elephants: A true story of animals, people, and war* (T. T. Dykes, Trans.). Boston, MA: Houghton Mifflin.

Tuchman, G. (2013). *Shark attack!* New York, NY: Scholastic.

Twain, M. (1884). *The adventures of Huckleberry Finn.* London, UK: Chatto & Windus.

Twain, M. (2001). *A Connecticut Yankee in King Arthur's court.* Mineola, NY: Dover. (Original work published 1889)

Twist, C. (2011). *A little book of slime: Everything that oozes, from killer slime to living mold.* New York, NY: Scholastic.

Vacca, R. T., & Vacca, J. L. (2007). *Content area reading: Literacy and learning across the curriculum* (9th ed.). Boston, MA: Allyn & Bacon.

Valencia, S. W., Wixson, K. K., & Pearson, P. D. (2014). Putting text complexity in context. *Elementary School Journal, 115*(2), 270–289.

Vonnegut, K. (1998). *Cat's cradle.* New York, NY: Dell.

Warren, A. (2004). *We rode the orphan trains.* New York, NY: HMH Books for Young Readers.

Weber, B. (2004). *Animal disguises.* London, UK: Kingfisher (Houghton Mifflin).

Wiesel, E. (1960). *Night* (S. Rodway, Trans.). New York, NY: Hill & Wang.

Wigfield, A., & Guthrie, J. T. (1997). Relations of children's motivation for reading to the amount and breadth of their reading. *Journal of Educational Psychology, 89*(3), 420–432.

Wulffson, D. (2000). *Toys! Amazing stories behind some great inventions.* New York, NY: Holt.

Yang, G. L. (2008). *American-born Chinese.* New York, NY: Square Fish.

Young, C., & Rasinski, T. (2009). Implementing readers theatre as an approach to classroom fluency instruction. *The Reading Teacher, 63*(1), 4–13.

Young, D. (2005). Annie Davis to Abraham Lincoln. In *Letters to the Oval Office* (p. 27). Washington, DC: National Geographic. (Original work published 1864)

Zeno, S., Ivens, S., Millard, R., & Duvvuri, R. (1995). *The educator's word frequency guide.* Brewster, NY: Touchstone Applied Science Associates.

Index

productive failure, 146
routines to support.
   See Collaborative instructional
   routines
supporting conditions, 145–146
text selection, 145
Peer-mediated learning. *See* Peer-led tasks
Peer talk, xiv
Peer tasks, 14–15
Personification, 53
Photo narratives, 154–155
Piaget, J., 83–84
Planning, 10
Pledge of Allegiance, 60
Poe, Edgar Allan, 112
Point of view, 53
Portmanteau words, 60
Practice effect, 161
Prior knowledge, 49, 62–63, 74, 87–88
Problem-and-solution text structure, 79
Procedural knowledge, 13
Productive failure, 16, 146
Programme for International Student
   Assessment (PISA), 32
Psycholinguistic measures, 35
Purpose:
   informational texts, 72, 76–77
   literary texts, 47, 54
   quantitative text measures, 39
   See also Levels of meaning and purpose

QAR. *See* Question–Answer Relationships
QR (quick response) codes, 152
Qualitative analysis:
   cautions about, 66–67
   informational text, 71–74
   literary texts, 45–50
Qualitative scale:
   informational text, 72–74
   literary texts, 47–49
Qualitative values:
   in *Hunger Games, The*, 64–66
   literary texts, 41–67
   overview, 5
Quantitative measures:
   cautions about quantitative analysis
      and, 36–37
   coreference and cohesion, 34–36
   defined, 23
   overview, 5
   sentence-level analysis, 25–26
   summary of, 39
   word-level analysis, 24–25
   See also Readability formulas

Question–Answer Relationships (QAR),
   171–173
Questions:
   student-teacher conferences, 171–174
   supporting analysis of how the
      text *works*, 120–124
   supporting analysis of what the
      text *means*, 124–126
   supporting analysis of what the
      text *says*, 117–120
   text-dependent, 117
Question the Author routine, 171–174
Quick response (QR) codes

RAND Reading Study Group, 3–5
Readability, 3
Readability formulas:
   Advantage-TASA Open Standard
      (ATOS), 29–30, 33
   Bormuth Readability Score, 31
   cautions about quantitative analysis of
      text, 36–37
   Coh-Metrix, 33, 35–36
   conventional, 27–30
   Degrees of Reading Power (DRP) tests,
      30–31, 33
   Flesch-Kincaid grade-level
      score, 29
   Flesch reading-ease score, 29
   Fry readability formula, 28–29
   history of, 23–24
   Lexile scale, 32–33
   quantitative measures, 23–39
   Reading Maturity Metric, 32, 33
   REAP, 33
   SourceRater, 31, 33
   summary of, 39
   TextEvaluator, 31–32
   that also assess readers, 30–33
Reader consideration, 21
Readers:
   characteristics of, checklist for, 11–12
   factors needed to understand, 6
   knowing how to read vs. being a reader,
      159–161
   tasks required of, 13–15
   teaching practices that
      motivate, 161
   traits of, 160
Reader's theater, 151–152
Reader–text relationships, 46
Reading, increasing. *See* Independent
   reading; Sustained silent reading
   (SSR)

BECAUSE ALL TEACHERS ARE LEADERS

A SAGE Company

Helping educators make the greatest impact

CORWIN HAS ONE MISSION: to enhance education through intentional professional learning.

We build long-term relationships with our authors, educators, clients, and associations who partner with us to develop and continuously improve the best evidence-based practices that establish and support lifelong learning.

INTERNATIONAL LITERACY ASSOCIATION

The International Literacy Association (ILA) is a global advocacy and membership organization with a network of more than 300,000 literacy educators, researchers, and experts across 75 countries. With over 60 years of experience, ILA has set the standard for how literacy is defined, taught, and evaluated. The mission of ILA is to empower educators, inspire students, and encourage leaders with the resources they need to make literacy accessible for all. For more information, visit literacyworldwide.org.